Holy Ghost

Holy Ghost

Decoding Leonardo da Vinci's Final Painting

Alex LaFollette

RESOURCE *Publications* · Eugene, Oregon

HOLY GHOST
Decoding Leonardo da Vinci's Final Painting

Resource Publications
An Imprint of Wipf and Stock Publishers
199 W. 8th Ave., Suite 3
Eugene, OR 97401

www.wipfandstock.com

PAPERBACK ISBN: 979-8-3852-4374-7
HARDCOVER ISBN: 979-8-3852-4375-4
EBOOK ISBN: 979-8-3852-4376-1

05/28/25

For Clara and Hugo.
There are many more mysteries to solve.

"It is a capital mistake to theorize before one has data. Insensibly one begins to twist facts to suit theories, instead of theories to suit facts."

Sir Arthur Conan Doyle,
The Adventures of Sherlock Holmes

Contents

CONTENTS

Acknowledgments

I AM DEEPLY GRATEFUL to the brilliant individuals and organizations whose generosity brought this book to life. Specifically, I would like to warmly thank Father Bradley Arturi, Michael Asciak, Carmen Bambach, Pierre Chamber-Protat, Marco Grilli, Martin Kemp, Erin LaFollette, Stephanie Welniak, and Frank Zöllner. Your time and expertise have been immeasurably valuable.

I also want to extend my heartfelt gratitude to the Knights of Malta, Opus Dei, and the Vatican Secret Archives for their benevolent support.

Introduction

OUR INDIVIDUALITY IS SHAPED by millennia of human history, molded further by modern environmental factors that influence our motivations. We do not choose our brains, our parents, the neighborhoods we grow up in, or the economic circumstances we face. Nor can we control the era we live in, our birthplace, or the events that happen and the events that do not happen to us. Yet these uncontrollable elements profoundly define who we become. Leonardo da Vinci, however, mastered his circumstances and thrived within these constraints. He was a product of his environment just as much as anyone else is. But despite his hardships early in life, he overcame them and flourished. Contrary to the common belief that he defied his era's rules, da Vinci excelled by understanding and navigating them, turning barriers into opportunities for greatness.

Saint John the Baptist was Leonardo da Vinci's final painting. But this painting transcends its surface to be more than a devotional portrait of a revered saint. It serves as a connection to a controversial and mysterious past. This story will make you uncomfortable. It will also challenge preconceived notions you have likely held for many years. Rooted in both mythical lore and an unnerving history, it upends what we thought we knew about the Renaissance. *Saint John the Baptist* is a vessel for ancient knowledge that reveals da Vinci's innermost thoughts. Beneath its outward depiction of a saint lies a revelation waiting to emerge. As with everything da Vinci had done, there are many hidden layers waiting to be discovered.

CHAPTER 1

The Gallows

MUCH OF THE RENAISSANCE was funded by the Medici family. This powerful household of bankers supported some of humanity's greatest artists including Michelangelo and Raphael. They were also major patrons of Leonardo da Vinci. While their wealth came from the banking industry, their involvement within their community yielded influence and support from the people. The House of Medici understood that to maintain power and control over Florence, they had to give their people something to be proud of. The arts were one way they did this. However, jealousy from other families emerged over the years, and some even took violent action to gain control. One of these plots came from the Pazzi household, a rival banking family. The Florentine Renaissance was a period of significant human advancement; it was also a time of great uncertainty. Ultimately, the Pazzi's attack on the Medicis failed.

On December 29th, 1479, a rope was tied around the neck of Bernardo Bandini dei Baroncelli. He, along with dozens of others, was found guilty of attempting to overthrow the Medici Family in Florence on behalf of the Pazzis. This revolt is known historically as the Pazzi Conspiracy. The background of this attack stems from the Pazzi Family carrying multiple gripes against the Medicis. Primarily, the Pazzis believed that the Medicis had too much control and influence over Florence, and they felt their status shrinking. However, the Pazzis were anything but weak. They even had the backing of Pope Sixtus IV due to his power struggles with Lorenzo de'

Medici. The Pazzis also believed they had enough support from the people of Florence. If the Pazzis could successfully overthrow the Medicis, then they would reign as the top banking family over all of Florence. At High Mass on Sunday, April 26th, 1478, they struck.

Lorenzo and his brother, Giuliano, went to the Duomo Cathedral for Mass. Giuliano de' Medici was attacked and ultimately killed by Bernardo Bandini dei Baroncelli and Francesco de' Pazzi at the church. Lorenzo was also attacked but Francesco Nori, a Florentine banker, aided Lorenzo in escaping. Nori found himself as the next best target and was killed at the church as well. The Pazzis hoped in vain that their assassination attempt against the Medicis would rile up the Florentine people to support them. The support never came. The assassinations backfired on the Pazzis. Roughly 80 people involved in the assassination were later executed, and any surviving Pazzi family members were forever banished from Florence. Despite the deaths of Giuliano de' Medici and Francesco Nori, the Medicis gained more support from the people of Florence. With the Pazzi family either dead or banished, Lorenzo de' Medici further consolidated his power.

Bernardo Bandini dei Baroncelli having been found guilty of assassinating Giuliano de' Medici and Francesco Nori was now to face the ultimate punishment. With a rope tightly tied around his neck, the floor below him disappeared and the life of Baroncelli came to a close. Among the people witnessing the hanging was Leonardo da Vinci. Still in his 20's, da Vinci pulled out his notebook and drew the hanging corpse. The quick, thin lines of the drawing, along with loose hatching for shading captured the image right in the moment. With the removal of the Pazzis, a new era was about to commence. A little more than a decade after the Pazzi Conspiracy, Florence entered what is now known as the High Renaissance, one of the greatest moments in human history. It was a time of invention, discovery, rediscovery, and art. Da Vinci's sketch of Baroncelli was a timestamp of this major shift.

The location of the hanging of Bernardo Bandini dei Baroncelli was at the Palazzo del Bargello. At the time it served as a public building and contained many works of art, some of which were depictions of Saint John the Baptist. One of those artworks is a sculpture made in the 1460's titled *Youthful Saint John the Baptist*. For years it was believed that Donatello was the artist behind the work, however, most art historians now believe the sculpture to have been by the hand of Desiderio da Settignano. Furthermore, the Palazzo del Bargello also has depictions of Dante Alighieri, author of the *Divine Comedy*, a personal favorite of Leonardo's. The *Divine Comedy* prominently features John the Baptist as well. Throughout da Vinci's life, both minor and major aspects of this one saint guided and inspired his work, ultimately leading to his final painting, *Saint John the Baptist*.

More than 500 years after the hanging of Baroncelli we are brought to the country of Malta where a different assassination occurred. Within this European nation is a tiny town called Bidnija. This little hamlet is one of the least populated areas in the entire country with only a few hundred people. Furthermore, it was never that remarkable in any historical sense. Its *claim to fame* is its olive tree grove which is over 5,000 years old. The olives growing there supply Malta with a resource for olive oil production. Another aspect of this town is that during World War II, when Malta was still a British colony, Bidnija manufactured rooms for soldiers, as well as war shelters for its citizens. Many of these structures remain there to this day. So, in all regards, this charming village existed in a seemingly tranquil, unnoticed corner of the world. This all changed when a Maltese journalist was heinously murdered there.

On October 16th, 2017, investigative journalist Daphne Caruana Galizia got into her Peugeot 108 and began driving. While on Triq il-Bidnija, a bomb attached to her car detonated, killing Galizia instantly. The blast essentially turned the vehicle into shrapnel, with tiny pieces of it being found nearly the length of an entire football field away. Her son Matthew was the one who located her bodily remains in a nearby field.[1] Malta is a hotbed for corruption. From 2016 to 2017 alone there were six car bombs, with Galizia's assassination being one of them.[2] However, the village of Bidnija had never experienced anything like that before. The people that live there rarely witness much crime at all, in part because of its minimal population. But suddenly Bidnija was making world news.

Daphne Galizia was a popular figure in Malta for her investigative journalism, which exposed corruption in the European nation. Her influence over the years expanded and her favor with the Maltese population rose. She was a dangerous person in the eyes of anyone operating in shady business dealings in Malta. Galizia also seemed bipartisan in her reporting, having gone after people of all political backgrounds. Considered a hero by

---

1. Galizia, "'I knew it was a car bomb straight away': the day my mother Daphne Caruana Galizia was murdered," lines 145–147.

2. Bonnici, "Daphne Caruana Galizia assassination: A week and a crime like no other," lines 3–5.

the public while she was alive, she was then elevated to the status of martyr through her death. People both inside, and outside of Malta, know about the corruption between its politicians, religious leaders, and businessmen. In this sparsely populated nation, speaking out can be dangerous, making an individual a clear target; just as it did with Galizia.

The response to the car bombing was intense. Daphne Galizia's family immediately blamed the Maltese government for being both negligent and responsible for her death. Maltese police officer, Sergeant Ramon Mifsud, posted a seemingly celebratory caption on his Facebook page following her assassination. The post was met with widespread condemnation.[3] Furthermore, it did not necessarily help with the image of the Maltese government and those in power, especially since Galizia had been critical of Mifsud in the past. It is essential to state that Mifsud had nothing to do with her death. Overall, social media was filled with overwhelming waves of support for Galizia and her family. Support was not confined to the sheltered walls of the internet, as citizens also took to the streets to show their support.

The assassination of this brave journalist further prompted public statements from world leaders to condemn the attack, as well as praising her work. Nationalist Party official, Adrian Delia, referred to Daphne Galizia as the last ethical voice in Malta.[4] Condemnation of the attack came from high-profile members of the European Commission, European Parliament, and many other powerful government organizations. Pope Francis wrote a condolence letter regarding the attack and stated he was praying for Galizia's family as well as the people of Malta.[5] The founder of WikiLeaks, Julian Assange, even offered a €20,000 reward for information that led to the arrest of her assassins.[6] Her death rocked the small island nation of Malta and highlighted the corruption that plagued it. People who had never heard of Malta before were now seeing it on the cover of every major news outlet.

Galizia was a prominent and fearless voice in investigative journalism. She became known throughout the nation for her pursuit of truth and her exposés on corruption, money laundering, and organized crime. Writing

3. Bonnici, "Daphne Caruana Galizia assassination: A week and a crime like no other," lines 127–130.

4. Delia, "The death of a crusading journalist rocks Malta," lines 6–9.

5. Henley, "Pope writes rare letter of condolence after murder of Daphne Caruana Galizia," line 1.

6. Assange, "Julian Assange offers €20k reward for information on Caruana Galizia murder," lines 11–12.

on various platforms, her blog was widely read and respected, including by top government officials. In the years leading up to her assassination, Galizia had been investigating several high-profile cases, including the Panama Papers scandal. This scandal implicated several prominent Maltese politicians, including then Prime Minister Joseph Muscat and his chief of staff, Keith Schembri. She was also investigating allegations of money laundering surrounding the illegal sales of Maltese passports to wealthy individuals. The car bomb attack that claimed Galizia's life was not only brutal and calculated but was also a stark reminder of the risks inherent in her work.

Investigative journalism is an essential component of a healthy democracy, as it utilizes free speech and freedom of the press to hold those in power accountable. However, this important work comes with significant risks, including violence. In many parts of the world, journalists who seek to expose corruption, human rights abuses, or other forms of wrongdoing are often made into targets. Intimidation, physical attacks, and murder are unfortunate realities. Violence is only one of many threats to investigative journalists. Legal threats are regularly used to silence reporters. In many countries, governments and powerful individuals use libel laws and other legal tools to silence journalists investigating wrongdoing. These lawsuits can be costly and time-consuming. They often have a chilling effect on other journalists considering similar investigations. At the time of Galizia's death, she was facing roughly 42 separate libel lawsuits.[7]

Yet another danger faced by investigative journalists is harassment. This can take many forms, from threats online to in-person intimidation. These challenges can weigh heavily on reporters and lead them to face significant psychological struggles. Not only that, but the results of their investigations can be emotionally taxing, especially when dealing with traumatic or disturbing subject matter. Furthermore, investigative journalists often face significant financial challenges. Investigative reporting is not only time-consuming but also expensive as it requires extensive resources and support. Many news organizations are reluctant to foot the bill for a journalist yearning to explore a story that might lead nowhere. Investigative journalism is a crucial component of a healthy democracy, but it comes with significant risks. These journalists face violence, legal threats, harassment, emotional and psychological challenges, financial constraints, and digital threats. Despite these dangers, many journalists pursue investigative

---

7. Bonnici, "Daphne Caruana Galizia's libel suits can still continue—lawyer Joseph Zammit Maempel," lines 4–5.

reporting, driven by a commitment to truth, justice, and accountability. Unfortunately, Galizia paid the ultimate price for her work.

Malta is a nation in which biblical legend states that the Apostle Paul arrived via shipwreck around 60 AD. Nearly 1,500 years after the shipwreck a Catholic chivalric order of warrior monks settled the land for themselves. This holy order has never dissolved and is still very much an active, influential group not only in Malta but throughout the world. Furthermore, Malta is friendly with a secretive and powerful Catholic organization that has a direct line to the Pope at the Vatican. Both organizations have deep connections to the people and government allegedly implicated in the assassination of Daphne Galizia. In addition, they have a deep veneration for John the Baptist, the subject of Leonardo da Vinci's final painting.

Throughout the case of Daphne Galizia, we will see a blurring of the lines between evidence and fantasy. Sifting through the material has made it difficult to understand if there was one, or multiple masterminds behind her death. This controversial investigative journalist in Malta made many of enemies. However, just because she made enemies with powerful people does not mean they all wanted her dead. Anyone can make accusations. But in the absence of clear evidence such claims are merely irresponsible, unsubstantiated allegations. Understanding this assassination requires grasping its many moving parts. It is crucial to consider not only the immediate causes, but also the broader context and circumstances that allowed the situation to develop. Malta is a nation under great influence from formidable groups. It is because of the power of these organizations that the public has been eager to place the blame on them. They may or may not be wrong.

CHAPTER 2

Secret Archives

THE FINAL PAINTING IN the life of Leonardo da Vinci was his *Saint John the Baptist*. This enigmatic work features Saint John with his right index finger pointing upwards towards the sky and his left index finger pointing towards his heart. He is androgynous in appearance, blurring the lines between masculine and feminine. Despite this, he is handsome, with long, curly hair past his shoulders. His body is almost completely naked, with only a small piece of clothing covering his lower stomach and genitals. A thin reed cross rests on him which assures the viewer that they indeed are looking at a rendition of John the Baptist. As with all da Vinci paintings, the sfumato technique is applied to eliminate harsh lines, creating a 3-dimensional aspect to his figure. Leonardo also utilized the chiaroscuro method which incorporates an all-black background to help illuminate John. In his *A Treatise on Painting*, da Vinci wrote extensively about the importance of incorporating light and shadow in works of art.

I was in my early twenties when I first saw the painting *Saint John the Baptist*. It didn't have a room full of admirers the same way that the *Mona Lisa* did. However, people still looked at the painting with great admiration. It was my first time leaving the country, and I took the trip alone. I was a recent university graduate, broke, and needed to see the world. So, I scraped together some money and booked the trip to Paris. It was the beginning of many other trips abroad for me. Da Vinci's painting of *Saint John the Baptist* was truly revolutionary as the saint had never been depicted in such a

way. In the Leonardo version, he is represented as a sex symbol. Mostly naked, with luscious hair, muscle definition, deep eyes, and an alluring smile.
While I stared at the painting in the Louvre it became apparent to me why
he depicted this important saint in such a specific manner. Now, more than
a decade later, I have set out to prove my theory.

Academic articles attempt to mitigate the problem of opinions being used as facts. However, this system is still flawed. I have had original
research of mine published in the past, so I am not coming at this from a
disgruntled, jaded point of view. Instead, I want to approach this as being
thoughtfully critical of a method in bed with academia. Reviewers, like everyone, carry biases. It is because of this that we see plagiarized and poorly
cited research papers still getting published. An example of this is the Clau-
dine Gay plagiarizing scandal.[1] It is overtly apparent that some researchers
have had their work approved despite their research not being of solid qual-
ity. The reason for this is if the analysis validates the reviewers' worldview,
then that paper has a better chance of getting the stamp of approval.

A notorious case that drew attention to the biases in academia was
the *Grievance Studies Affair*. Three researchers, Peter Boghossian, James A.
Lindsay, and Helen Pluckrose, teamed up to write a series of incredibly
over-the-top, fictionalized, and politically biased *scholarly* papers. Their
goal was to see if they could publish any of them in an academic journal. To
their astonishment, four papers were officially published, and another three
were accepted for various journals. The reason why the three that were only
accepted but never published is most likely because their operation had
been exposed by that point. To highlight how bizarre these hoax articles
were, some of their topics included exploring themes of *rape culture at dog
parks*, and *fat bodybuilding*. Once the hoax was made public, their mission
was applauded by notable figures like Richard Dawkins and Steven Pinker.
This example shows the widespread political bias that fogs the lenses of
academia.

Plenty of issues with real academic papers also need to be addressed.
The main one to mention is the amount of pressure an academic reviewer
might encounter. Is a 28-year-old peer reviewer really going to reject a
study submitted by an older, tenured professor with hundreds of published
studies under her belt? Probably not. Cronyism is another element that
plagues research. What I mean by this is that it is common for researchers
to review and publish each other's work for various journals. A type of *if*

---

1. Chaaraoui, "A Conversation with Dr. Carol Swain," lines 1–9.

you publish mine, I'll publish yours approach. And *blind peer review* is not always as blind as you might think. If heavily flawed, but still popular research is published it can create a snowball effect. Retracting faulty research is not enough as it may have already been cited in hundreds of other papers. There is also classic retaliation. Publishing research that goes against the status quo can carry consequences, as suggested by Roland Fryer.[2]

A fair amount of social science research is simply just political activism, which strongly resembles religion as observed by people such as John McWhorter. This dogmatic approach stems from the disciples of post-modern thinkers Michel Foucault and Jacques Derrida. If you push back, then you run the risk of being shunned by the insulated academic community. In other words, researchers can be excommunicated for blasphemy. Another example of these religious overtones is scholars telling non-academics that they cannot interpret *academic speech*. Because of this, they say that they need to translate the research to then tell them what to think about it. This is like priests telling their congregation that since they do not know Latin, they'll translate the meaning of it on their behalf. The parallels between religion and the modern social sciences are astounding.

The 2016 study "Neural correlates of maintaining one's political beliefs in the face of counterevidence," co-authored by Sam Harris, further shows how personal emotions and beliefs are not likely to change, even when presented with strong counterevidence. *These results highlight the role of emotion in belief-change resistance and offer insight into the neural systems involved in belief maintenance, motivated reasoning, and related phenomena.*[3] We can all find a relevant study to back our position, but these studies likely will not sway other people's opinion. *You have your studies, and I have mine.* It is important to remember the next time you hurl a study at someone you disagree with that it may later become one of the more than 10,000 a year that gets retracted.[4] At the very least, you should know who wrote it, who reviewed it, who financed it, and what the purpose was behind it. What you find may shock you. We need experts, but we must also be prudent.

---

2. McDonald, "Prof says 'all hell broke loose' at Harvard after his study found no racial bias in police shootings," lines 40–67.

3. Harris, "Neural correlates of maintaining one's political beliefs in the face of counterevidence," lines 10–12.

4. McKie, "'The situation has become appalling': fake scientific papers push research credibility to crisis point," lines 6–8.

Approaching a singular painting by a Renaissance artist inherently poses significant challenges. The first is the absurd amount of myth surrounding Leonardo da Vinci. It amazes me how many people attribute the most unserious claims to da Vinci while displaying the most serious of faces. Describing a work of art usually requires no more than a few paragraphs, which is generous. Being an art critic requires incredible skill, but rarely, if ever, requires sources. So, decoding the meaning behind da Vinci's *Saint John the Baptist* demands a thoughtful approach. In addition, understanding the influence that John the Baptist had during the Renaissance helps to build evidence. I knew that I was about to swim in a sea of primary and secondary sources. Therefore, I jumped right in and was lucky to have received assistance from the Vatican Apostolic Archives.

Up until 2019, the Vatican Apostolic Archives was known as the Vatican Secret Archives. This original naming structure presents an aura of mystery surrounding it. But it needs to be mentioned that the word *secret* carried a different meaning in centuries past. When translated into Latin, the linguistical structure of the word *secret* loosely translates to meaning personal property rather than something withheld from others. In the 1960's, the *secret* name was still merited as the cataloging system. This was because the records were so ancient and orderless that it was like how an archeology dig was secret.[5] Fortunately, much of this work has now been cataloged, so the ancient understanding of the word *secret* does not necessarily apply anymore. Additionally, many of these documents are digitally archived for scholars to access more easily.

The Vatican Apostolic Archives technically dates to the 1st century when the early Christians began compiling documentation. These records stayed under the protection and possession of religious leaders, including popes. However, popes were required to do a great deal of travel, and some of the first popes traveled with these records in hand. This risky strategy led to many of these documents becoming lost.[6] Because of this problem, the documents were stored at Lateran Palace, and then shortly thereafter were stored within the official papal residence.[7] It was not until the year 1612 when Pope Paul V ordered all Church records to be stored in one location. Despite a bout with Napoleon ordering the archives to be stored in Paris in 1809 (they were later returned in 1814), the archives have remained in

---

5. Ambrosini, *The Secret Archives of the Vatican*, 16.

6. Ambrosini, *The Secret Archives of the Vatican*, 27.

7. Ambrosini, *The Secret Archives of the Vatican*, 134.

Vatican City. These documents are some of the most sought-after records in history.

Dr. Pierre Chambert-Protat, reference librarian at the Vatican Apostolic Archives, was kind enough to assist me with my research. He stressed to me that the only documentation they have of Saint John the Baptist were copies of the New Testament. He was confident in his assertion because of the sheer number of researchers who reviewed the documents held there. I have every reason to believe him. Dr. Marco Grilli, the secretary to the prefecture of the Archives, also provided me with information. He pointed out that even though much of the cataloging for the Archives has been completed, it is not alphabetized. This, compounded with many of these documents being in Latin and Italian, adds complexity. However, Dr. Grilli was kind enough to provide me with several digital archives to review. The documents were the *Die Register Innocenz' III*, *Regesta Honorii papae III di P. Pressutti*, and the *Regestum Clementis papae V*. It was the latter document that brought me to a conflict that began several hundred years before the birth of da Vinci: The Crusades.

CHAPTER 3

The Knights Templar

To TRULY UNDERSTAND LEONARDO da Vinci's motivations behind his *Saint John the Baptist* painting, we must look further into the past. Many angles need to be taken to fully comprehend such an old painting, particularly ones with little documentation. Simply looking at the visuals of the artwork, how it was made, and the biblical passages it may, or may not, reference is not enough. Da Vinci's depiction of Saint John the Baptist pointing upwards toward the sky is straightforward. However, da Vinci's paintings are not that easy to interpret, and this one is no different. A major question that arises with the *Saint John the Baptist* painting is why he is depicted in such a radical way. There needs to be a holistic approach to decode what is truly being said in the work. Because of this, we must go back a few hundred years before the birth of Leonardo da Vinci.

The Crusades were one of the most contentious moments in history. Its first military campaigns began in 1096 under Pope Urban II, and the Catholics were victorious in their conquest of Jerusalem in 1099. It sparked a series of on-and-off conflicts that lasted for hundreds of years. As with any large-scale war, there are several complex reasons for the fighting. Some nuanced reasons include, but are not limited to, Christian versus Muslim tensions, belief in an upcoming apocalypse, as well as feudalist land grabs. These are well-documented assertions that play a role in the cause of the Crusades. However, the origin of the war was to protect Christian pilgrims with safe passage to the Holy Land. Catholics were incentivized to fight because they were told they were fighting on behalf of God and that it was an act of penance.[1] Catholic leaders also stressed to recruits that Jesus Christ and John the Baptist did not outright condemn violence and acknowledged the necessity of soldiers.[2]

Compelling arguments have been made that Jesus advocated for pacifism, which has inspired several Christian sects. In addition, prominent individuals such as Martin Luther King Jr. and Leo Tolstoy were directly inspired by pacifist texts found in the Bible. This is, however, far from both the traditional and modern understanding of Christianity. Religious leaders and scholars have pointed to quotations from Jesus and other characters in the New Testament that contradict outright pacifist claims. One example is when Christ physically banished the moneychangers from the Temple. This has not only been viewed as justified violence but also as righteous anger from the mainstream Christian perspective. It should also go without saying that the Old Testament is filled with varying degrees of violence, often done under the direct commandment of God.

So even with moments in Christian history of pacifism, or pacifistic elements, anti-war sentiment was not the mainstream. There is very little documentation of any Christian being against the Crusades. They were instructed to help Christian pilgrims enter the Holy Land in one piece, and they were willing to do whatever was needed to make that happen. History is complex and it can seem like the easy way out to say that these Christians were hypocrites for taking part in the Crusades. The truth is pacifism was rarely a driving force in the history of Christianity. There are, of course, biblical passages that cite the necessity of peace. But just as those passages exist, so do passages that permit the use of force over certain matters. Approaching the Crusades with the assumption that Catholics were hypocritical about war will hinder a clear understanding of this ancient conflict.

After Jerusalem was secured by Catholic forces many other regions were still under attack. This was the main culprit that led to the Crusades becoming an ongoing conflict. It incurred high enlistment rates, as well as outside supporters with varying personal motivations. The Middle East has long been a hotbed of conflict before, during, and after the Crusades, and its present-day is heavily connected to its past. A war with a singular focus on protecting Christian pilgrims was compounded with individual and political desires, and religion was used as the backdrop for all of this. There

1. Riley-Smith, *The Crusades, Christianity, and Islam*, 9.
2. Riley-Smith, *The Crusades, Christianity, and Islam*, 11.

are many approaches a historian can take when assessing the Crusades. One concept that historians of all backgrounds tend to share regarding this is that it was incredibly messy. Through this chaotic history, several high-profile military orders emerged from the Crusades. The Knights Templar is probably the most well-known.

During the nearly 200 years of their existence, the Knights Templar were able to operate in secrecy while maintaining public support. But it was their secret nature that ultimately caused their disbandment and later their manufactured lore. They were a highly skilled Catholic military order created to protect pilgrims on their way to the Holy Land. Because of this, we can see why positive rumors swirled about the Templars from Catholics. Historically these pilgrims would come under brutal attacks from Muslim forces, and now safe passages had been provided to them. These warrior monks had initiation ceremonies and followed strict protocols in their daily lives. Popes and kings found them useful not only because of their military prowess but also because they were a symbol of projecting Christian strength.

Baldwin IV of Jerusalem, also known as Baldwin the Leper, was a young king who reigned from 1174 to 1185. He had a resurgence in popularity over the actor Edward Norton's depiction of him in the 2005 Ridley Scott film, Kingdom of Heaven. In the movie, he wears a silver, metal-appearing mask to hide his deformities. While Baldwin IV certainly had leprosy, no records of him ever wearing a mask to cover it exist. He is best known for his courage and military brilliance and defending off foes with great strength. Being well-known as an ambitious aggressor and staunch defender of Jerusalem, he gained immense loyalty and support from his followers. This boosted the power of the Catholic Crusaders and created not only influence but also myth from Christians. Baldwin IV of Jerusalem was a strong collaborator and supporter of the Knights Templar which helped to increase their power.

King Baldwin IV's arguably most famous battle was the Battle of Montgisard in 1177. Fought between the Ayyubid Dynasty and the Kingdom of Jerusalem, a 16-year-old Baldwin IV led his troops, which included 80 Knights Templar members, to an important victory. The heart of the triumph lay in King Baldwin IV attacking Saladin's embarrassingly ill-prepared troops.[3] Saladin himself seemed to have narrowly escaped the incoming barrage. This triumph created greater power for the Christian

---

3. Lane-Pool, *Saladin and the Fall of the Kingdom of Jerusalem*, 154–55.

Crusaders and is remembered to this day as a great victory. The conflict, however, was incredibly bloody, and both sides suffered mass devastation. Roger de Moulins, eighth Grand Master of the Order of Knights of the Hospital of Saint John the Baptist of Jerusalem, was a close confidante to King Baldwin IV, and their troops regularly fought side by side. It was his reporting that stated there were over 1,100 deaths and 750 injuries on the side of the Christians.[4]

The Knights Templar, whose official name was *Poor Fellow-Soldiers of Christ and of the Temple of Solomon*, was a real military order that was also saturated by myth. Their stated goal was to defend Christian pilgrims from attacks by Muslims while traveling to the Holy Land. Founded around 1118, this military order grew rapidly and became incredibly wealthy, powerful, and popular. During its early years of formation, the Vatican stressed the importance of love within the brotherhood. Pope Innocent II likened this love to inspire the Knights Templar. He connected this bond to the words in the Gospel of John to lay down their life for those closest to them to show great love.[5] This greatly strengthened these Christian warriors as they gained support and notoriety.

Pseudo-academic research, entertainment, video games, and more have presented the Knights Templar as an almost mystical order. Some suggestions about the military order are that they were in possession of the Holy Grail. Another is that they protected the bloodline of Jesus Christ. And a third one is that members still exist to this very day. All of this is not only over-romanticized but outright false. Even if these proposals are true, there is no speck of currently known evidence to substantiate the claims. No documentation, pottery, weaponry, or any evidence at all linking the Knights Templar to any of this. Myths tend to develop around great people or influential groups, and the history of the Knights Templar is not immune to this. Approaching their history in a responsible, prudent manner is the only way to provide us with an accurate view.

Another aspect of lore that needs to be addressed is the Priory of Sion. Rumors have run rampant that this is a real secret society that dates to 1099 and protects important religious information. Claims have been made that Sir Isaac Newton, Leonardo da Vinci, and the Knights Templar were involved in this organization. The reality is that there is no serious

---

4. Stevenson, *Crusaders in the East: A Brief History of the Wars of Islam with the Latins in Syria During the Twelfth and Thirteenth Centuries*, 218.

5. Riley-Smith, *Crusades, Christianity, and Islam*, 21.

documentation, or evidence, for any of these claims. In the French town of Saint-Julien-en-Genevois, Pierre Plantard created the Priory of Sion in 1956 in an attempt to create a new chivalric order. However, it was only a trivial organization that demanded cheaper housing and lambasted their local government.[6] It dissolved the same year that it was founded. Plantard later tried to link the Priory of Sion to an ancient royal network by manufacturing forged documents. The Priory of Sion was an elaborate lie, and there is no legitimate connection to this hoax with the Knights Templar.

What is factual, and important to mention regarding the Templars, is that they were incredibly disciplined, and their standards were high. The *Latin Rule* was a document with 72 clauses that aimed at keeping its members accountable for their actions. It borrowed from the *Rule of Saint Augustine* and was further inspired by the *Rule of Saint Benedict*. Originally written in 1128, some of these rules included eating meat in moderation, bathing with permission, and board games were strictly forbidden.[7] It would be far-fetched to believe that the Templars followed these rules all the time. However, it does stress the rigorous criteria set out for them, especially regarding other Crusaders. It also helped to create a public persona for the Knights Templar.

Symbolism is a longstanding component of being human. We look for symbols to represent both our feelings and reality, as well as to confirm our own belonging. Universities, militaries, sports organizations, and more, use symbols to help identify one another. While entertaining conspiracies can run wild regarding the Knights Templar, their symbols carry no deeper meaning than what we already know them to be. An example is that of their seal which includes two men riding the same horse. While this is certainly open to varying interpretations, the common understanding is that it was meant to represent their devotion to poverty in the service of God. It can be tempting to place a secret, mystical theory to the Knights Templar, especially with their use of symbolism. But it must be remembered that at their peak they had a membership of around 20,000 soldiers. That is simply too many people in an organization to hold a powerful secret.

If there was a powerful, dark secret that the Knights Templar held, despite having tens of thousands of members, we do not have any evidence for it. But if one existed with the Templars then two likely outcomes could

---

6. Chaumeil, *Table d'Isis ou Le Secret de la Lumière, Editions Guy Trédaniel*, 121–24.

7. Holland, "Knights Templar Rulebook Included No Pointy Shoes and No Kissing Mom," line 1.

have happened. The first outcome is that the secret eventually would have come out. The Templars existed for nearly 200 hundred years and not a single member said, wrote, or left a clue anywhere to be found of an important secret. The second option is that they took this secret with them to the grave. But this brings us back to the first option as to why did they then not leave clues for the secret to later be found? Why let the secret die with them? The answer is because there is no secret. There is not a single ounce of evidence, or anything to suggest that the Knights Templar did anything more than what we already know about them.

The Knights Templar did have many spiritual influences, one of them being Saint John the Baptist. One of their seals even featured the prophet, which further highlights his importance to the Templars. They also had instructions to fast at the vigils of the twelve Apostles, as well as at the vigil of Saint John the Baptist.[8] Large-scale, mass conversions were not common during the Crusades. And since the primary goal of this ancient conflict was territorial conquest, forced conversions in general were not a focus of the Knights Templar. With that being said, baptisms into the Catholic faith did play a role, including in the working vicinities of the Knights Templar.[9] This further adds to the perceived connection that the Templars had to the saint.

During their military campaigns, the Knights Templar established fortresses and occupied various structures in the region where John the Baptist resided. One of these examples is the Al-Aqsa Mosque in Jerusalem, which was Templar headquarters. The Templars also built castles and outposts along and near the Jordan River which is the location where John the Baptist baptized Jesus. Additionally, they had a significant influence on the town of Sebaste, which Catholic tradition states is where the headless body of John the Baptist was laid to rest. This is one of the many regions where the Templars protected Catholics on their pilgrimages to holy sites for adoration. Crusaders even fortified a Byzantine Basilica over the supposed tomb of John the Baptist. This Crusader church was named the Cathedral of Saint John the Baptist, but Muslim warriors later converted the cathedral into a mosque. The Knights Templar had a deep, inspirational devotion to John the Baptist; however, it was not one of worship. Nevertheless, the influence of John the Baptist was ultimately used against them as they met a fiery demise.

---

8. Upton-Ward, *Rule of the Templars*, 37.

9. Babcock, *History of Deeds Done Beyond the Sea*, 392.

CHAPTER 4

Downfall

IN EGYPT IN 1945, a farmer named Muhammed al-Samman discovered thirteen ancient papyrus documents that were leatherbound and protected by a jar. These old documents forever changed how we look at the traditional Bible and the early Christians. Officially known as the Nag Hammadi Library, based on the village in which they were found, they are more popularly called the Gnostic Gospels. Currently in possession of the Coptic Museum in Cairo, these are some of the authenticated gospels rejected from entering the official biblical canon. Over 50 gospels exist within this collection. Some of them include the Gospel of Thomas and the Gospel of Philip. There is widespread debate among academics as to which non-canonical gospels should be considered Gnostic and which ones should not be. There is even debate as to who the Gnostics were. However, for the sake of clarity moving forward, all non-canonical gospels mentioned will be referred to as Gnostic Gospels.

The Gospel of Philip is estimated to have been written sometime in the 3rd century, and possibly even earlier. As with the four officially recognized gospels of the Bible, Matthew, Mark, Luke, and John, we do not know who the author of the Gospel of Philip was. But inside this infamous text are writings that directly discuss a close relationship between Mary Magdalene and Jesus Christ. Specifically, it discusses how Mary Magdalene was regularly at his side and that he had a unique preference for her.[1] It also refers to her as his *koinōnos*, a Coptic word for companion. Traditionally in the Bible, this further translates to mean *spouse* as it is read in Malachi 2:14 and 3 Maccabees 4:6. Even more shocking, the Gospel of Philip says that Jesus regularly kissed Mary Magdalene. Is it too much of a stretch to suggest that Jesus was married? This premise further alludes to Jesus establishing a bloodline by having children. In recent decades, conspiracy theories have flourished over this thought. There are more ancient gospels worth mentioning that further explore this premise.

In 1896, the Gospel of Mary was unearthed. Religious scholar, Bart Ehrman points out that in this document the Apostle Levi says that Jesus Christ loved Mary Magdalene more than any other disciple of his.[2] While it seems outlandish for Jesus to have been married and fathered children, it should also be remembered that the Gospels of Matthew, Mark, Luke, and John contain eccentric stories as well. One of many examples is the traditionally told Nativity Story. This strange story states that Caesar Augustus required every citizen of the Roman Empire to register for a census, which forced Mary and Joseph to travel great lengths. The problem with this story is that there is no documentation or evidence whatsoever of this demand outside of the Gospel of Luke. The Romans never demanded a census of this sort in the history of their existence that required such strenuous travel. Even if the travel demands were met, the Roman authorities would have no way of confirming every citizen's identity.

The Gospel of Judas is another Gnostic Gospel and was discovered in Egypt in the 1970's. This document tells the story of Jesus' crucifixion through a defense of Judas. In the Bible, Judas is the one who betrays Jesus to the Romans. However, in the Gospel of Judas, which was written sometime before 180 AD, it is claimed that Judas was not a villain, but rather a divine human that Jesus gives secret teachings to. This Gnostic Gospel presents Judas as a hero and challenges the traditional Christian understanding of him. At the beginning of the Gospel of Judas, Jesus claims that he can be found among his followers as a child. This has led to further speculative theories that Jesus Christ established a bloodline. It also gives us a deeper insight into the beliefs of the early Christians.

At best, the earliest of the four traditionally accepted gospels was the Book of Mark which was most likely written around 70 AD. This means

1. Isenberg, *Gospel of Philip*, 139.
2. Ehrman, *Lost Scriptures*, 35.

that the oldest known gospel was written, at the earliest, around 35 years after the crucifixion of Jesus Christ. This is an incredible amount of time to have passed since his death and resurrection. Christian apologists often state that oral traditions were much stronger back then when compared to modern times. They are correct. However, there are countless examples of other oral traditions around that period that clearly show great manipulation, one example being the story of *Romulus and Remus*. The Gospel of John is the last written canonical Gospel having been completed between 90 AD and 110 AD. Certain Gnostic Gospels, like the Gospel of Thomas, were written around the same time as the Gospel of John, and possibly even earlier.

The Gnostic oral traditions are dated much further back than their official writings. You cannot claim that one oral tradition is stronger than another oral tradition just because it contradicts your own belief system. Biblical scholar, Richard Valantasis, states that the earliest written aspects of the Gospel of Thomas begin as early as 60 AD.[3] This would mean that the Gospel of Thomas could potentially rival the Gospel of Mark, the Bible's oldest canonical gospel. It also proves that the oral tradition for this text is older than 60 AD. Another gripping element to the Gospel of Thomas is that it mentions Mary Magdalene as being one of the closest disciples to Jesus Christ. The other characters in this text even seem to be slightly annoyed with her consistent presence next to him. Again, no text explicitly states that they were married. However, texts such as these make for a plausible scenario. Her prominence is so high in the Bible and Gnostic Gospels that historians confidently place her with having her own apostolic ministry following Christ's crucifixion.[4]

It is a common misconception that there was some theoretical force-field that only allowed for Matthew, Mark, Luke, and John to have been written. This could not be further from the truth. There were many competing ideologies that gained traction from both oral traditions and as a written record. Early Christians, living decades after the death of Christ were left with a great amount of freedom for creating and attributing myth to their Messiah. We see this attempt written in the canonical gospels, and we also see it in the Gnostic ones. Linguist and translator, Thomas Lambdin, translated the Gospel of Thomas. The end of this gospel is peculiar as Jesus tells his disciples that the Kingdom of God is already here for those

---

3. Valantasis, *Gospel of Thomas*, 20.
4. Price, "Mary Magdalene: Gnostic Apostle," lines 86–97.

who understand the cosmological secrets. Jesus also says in this gospel that the only way to reach Heaven is to be male.[5]

> *(113) His disciples said to him, "When will the kingdom come?" Jesus said, "It will not come by waiting for it. It will not be a matter of saying 'here it is' or 'there it is.' Rather, the kingdom of the father is spread out upon the earth, and men do not see it."*
> *(114) Simon Peter said to him, "Let Mary leave us, for women are not worthy of life." Jesus said, "I myself shall lead her in order to make her male, so that she too may become a living spirit resembling you males. For every woman who will make herself male will enter the kingdom of heaven."*

Another Gnostic Gospel is the Pistis Sophia, which was discovered in 1773 and written sometime between the 3rd and 4th centuries. The Pistis Sophia shares the same concepts among other Gnostic Gospels regarding the Divine Feminine. This was viewed by the ancients as the female counterpart to Jesus Christ. While they did not view Sophia as being on the same level as Jesus, they did view her as his counterpart in the sense of being the Bride of Christ. It is difficult for historians to decipher if the Bride of Christ was meant to be taken literally by the Gnostics or not. But regardless, this has further fueled speculation of Jesus having been married. This ancient text also deals with several controversial themes such as Jesus remaining on earth after his resurrection to discuss the lowest and highest cosmological mysteries with his disciples. The Pistis Sophia places Mary Magdalene as one of Jesus' most important disciples, which further adds even more to the lore of marriage and children between the two.

One of the eerie similarities between many of the Gnostic Gospels is the Five Seals. This is a baptismal rite involving immersion-style baptism in holy water 5 times in a row. It furthers the importance and influence of John the Baptist, even among the early, more mystical Christians. Mentioned both directly and indirectly in many Gnostic Gospels, he is presented as a key figure in the faith. The ritual of the Five Seals is mentioned in the Apocryphon of John, the Holy Book of the Great Invisible Spirit, the Trimorphic Protennoia, and the Zostrianos. In the Zostrianos, the main figure is baptized multiple times and becomes several versions of an angel. This theology departs from the mainstream Christian narrative of the reason for baptism. In Christianity, baptism is meant to wash away Original Sin and prepare the faithful for Heaven. However, in the

---

5. Lambdin, *Gospel of Thomas*, 11–12.

Zostrianos, baptism offers the potential to become an angel that can travel through the levels of the cosmos.

The Gnostic Gospels predate the standardized Christian Bible by centuries. The 27 books of the New Testament were not even explicitly listed as a canon until 367 by Athanasius of Alexandria. Another essential date is 405 when Saint Jerome created the Vulgate. This was a Latin translation of the Bible that standardized the Old and New Testaments, becoming the authoritative text for the Western Church. Before the Vulgate, Christians relied on individual holy texts, not always viewing them as a cohesive unit. Many of these early Christians were also incorporating Gnostic Gospels. Saint Jerome's work brought clarity to the faith by his consolidation. But even after the creation of the Vulgate, many early Christians were still following Gnostic scripture. This persisted until orthodox leaders, through debates and councils, gradually phased them out in favor of canonical texts. Docetism was a prominent Christian movement founded between 90 and 120 AD, which did not believe Jesus existed in physical, human form. Following Gnostic texts such as the Gospel of Peter, these Christians believed Christ was pure spirit, and therefore did not suffer on the Cross. Efforts such as the Vulgate sought to gradually remove these religious ideologies.

These ancient Gnostic Gospels and the theories that have emanated from them in recent years have led some to believe these texts carry secret truths. The Knights Templar is included in this type of storytelling because their demise was so abrupt and brutal that it can be hard to fathom the mainstream narrative as fact. This is why some people likened these Gnostic Gospels with the concept of a Holy Grail, and that the Knights Templar were the ones protecting this powerful secret. It is because they possessed this hidden knowledge that they were tortured and disbanded. Legend further states that the Knights Templar managed to hold on to this secret and pass it down over generations. At one point, this secret Holy Grail landed in the possession of Leonardo da Vinci in which he left secret codes in his artwork to later be discovered.

The reality is that the Knights Templar were disbanded for various political and financial reasons. All of this has been extensively documented. It isn't even known if any of the thousands of Templars that existed knew about the Gnostic Gospels, or if they were aware of a concept of a Holy Grail. Additionally, Leonardo da Vinci may not have been aware of the Gnostic Gospels or a Holy Grail either. And if he left any secret codes behind, they would have been discovered by now. Da Vinci did not even seem to be that interested in pursuing religious mystical secrets in his life either. In his notebooks, Leonardo even wrote, . . .*The rest of the definition of the soul I leave to the minds of the friars, the fathers of the people, who know all secrets by inspiration. I leave the sacred books alone because they are the supreme truth.*[6]

The Knights Templar was a Chivalric Order of military monks that fought in the Crusades. No evidence suggests they ever came across these Gnostic Gospels, much less believed in them. Even if they did come across some or all of them, we do not have credible evidence as to how they perceived them. Without an established understanding of the Templars and the Gnostic Gospels, the theory of them protecting the Holy Grail and Christ's bloodline begins to unravel. In addition, it destroys any argument about this information being passed down to Leonardo da Vinci. However, there is evidence we do have that draws a direct line between the Knights Templar, Leonardo da Vinci, and John the Baptist. These connections become apparent with the fiery demise of the Knights Templar.

During their almost 200 years of operation, the Knights Templar became increasingly wealthy and influential. The Crusades were a popular campaign, and the notion of a high-profile military order added to the allure. Think of how American special operation forces such as the Green Berets or the Navy Seals carry a good deal of popularity. The Templars were no different, except instead of existing for a few decades and serving one's country, the Templars had been around for hundreds of years and served God. They were a holy military order protecting the Holy Land and the Christians that traveled or lived there. A period without any technology also meant that legends around them were easily built. Ultimately this backfired on the Templars as they rose through the ranks of power and fame.

Philip IV was the King of France and reigned from 1285–1314. Known as the Iron King, Philip IV looked to bring France into an age of an early modern state, rather than a feudal one. One of the ways he did this was by increasing his power as a monarch and limiting feudal entitlements.[7] This was not necessarily a revolutionary move, but it was signaling the beginning of a new era to steer Europe out of the Dark Ages. When he took the throne he inherited the debt of his father, King Philip III of France, from wars in Aragon.[8] In fact, by 1286 he had owed the Templars

---

6. Baring, *Thoughts on Art and Life by Leonardo da Vinci*, 17.

7. Strayer, *Reign of Philip the Fair*, xiii.

8. Strayer, *Reign of Philip the Fair*, 11.

what was roughly seventeen percent of his entire government's revenue. He was eventually able to swiftly pay off these debts and operate on a surplus.[9] However, finances continued to be held over King Philip IV, particularly with the ongoing Crusades. This paired with him looking to move away from feudalism added unique complexities to his reign. Because of this, King Philip IV looked to bring an end to the Knights Templar.

Claims have been made that money is the central reason why people commit bad acts. However, this is not entirely true. Plenty of actions, both noble and immoral, have occurred without any financial motivation behind them. Money can play a role in actions, but not always. We are complex creatures and cannot be reduced to existing for pure financial reasons. So, while it is true that King Philip IV was indebted to the Knights Templar, this is not the entire story. Political sway and influence played just as, if not more, a prominent role than finances. I am not suggesting that finances didn't matter during King Philip's reign. But if King Philip IV lost his authority because of owing money to the Knights Templar, then he would have had much bigger issues to worry about.

In the mid-twelfth century, Muslim forces became much more powerful under their leader, Saladin. Christian Crusaders had been pushed back in various areas and suffered mighty losses. The Templars also reportedly clashed with other Catholic military orders. This infighting did not help them with the rise of opposing forces. After losing a few campaigns they were forced out of several of their headquarters. By the early 1300's, the Crusaders lost their stronghold in the Holy Land. Even though support for the Crusaders and the Knights Templar began decreasing during this time, the Templars were still an important fixture of daily life for Catholics.[10] Without a clear military campaign but simultaneously holding great influence over the life of peasants, Pope Clement V became weary of their wandering power. In 1305, Pope Clement V proposed merging the Templars with the Knights Hospitaller of Saint John the Baptist. Neither side agreed to the idea.

The combination of King Philip IV owing money to the Templars, and Pope Clement V being hesitant with their growing fame despite losing recent battles, proved fatal. It was ultimately decided by the Pope and

---

9. Torre, *Monetary Fluctuations in Philip IV's Kingdom of France and Their Relevance to the Arrest of the Templars*. In Jochen Burgtorf; Paul F. Crawford & Helen Nicholson (eds.). *The Debate on the Trial of the Templars (1307–1314)*, 59.

10. Nicholson, *Knights Templar: A New History*, 5.

King that action needed to be taken. In 1307, on Friday the 13th of October, King Philip IV ordered the arrest of the Knights Templar and their 23rd Grand Master, Jacques de Molay. A problem though is that the Knights Templar could not simply be arrested because a king owed them money. They also couldn't be taken down because a pope was insecure about their influence. So instead, fabricated charges were hurled against them. Some of these charges included spitting on the Cross and worshipping idols.[11] This quickly turned the tide of public support against the Templars as many of the Knights confessed to these allegations. The issue with the confessions is that they were done under duress because they were tortured.

An allegation against the Knights Templars was that they worshipped a demon named Baphomet, or a severed head that they kept with them. Some scholars believe this refers to the head of Saint John the Baptist.[12] Charges against the Templars include the denial of Jesus and the saints, including John the Baptist. They were then accused of claiming that Christ was a false prophet, and that salvation could not be reached through him. This includes John the Baptist because baptism is a way to cleanse your sins and prepare your soul for Christ. The Templars were further accused of homosexual acts. This is imperative to know because Leonardo da Vinci was a gay man once charged with soliciting a male prostitute. Da Vinci very well could have sympathized with them over this charge. Another major charge was that they did not believe in the Catholic sacraments, which included baptism.[13] There is no proof that any of these accusations were true. However, this was not common knowledge to the people at the time.

The allegations made against the Templars aligned with what the Cathars believed. Catharism was a minor Christian movement that was denounced by the Catholic Church. There were many elements to Cathar beliefs, including that Jesus was not man-made and therefore unable to have been crucified. Because of this the Cathars did not hold the Cross in high regard and were often accused of abusing it. It just so happens that disrespecting the Cross was a charge levied against the Templars. This further added an emotional element as Muslim warriors were known to drag the Cross along the ground before battling Crusaders. The Cathars also refused to partake in baptism by water. Connecting the Templars to Catharism

11. Riley-Smith, *Oxford Illustrated History of the Crusades*, 213.

12. Edgeller, *Taking the Templar Habit: Rule, Initiation Ritual, and the Accusations Against the Order*, 62–66.

13. Barber, *Trial of the Templars*, 178.

proved to be enough for Pope Clement V and King Philip IV to bring them down, even if none of it was true.[14]

Through torture, false confessions, and a sham trial, the Templars were found guilty of heresy. After the trials against the Knights Templar, some were ultimately freed and went on to serve in other military orders, retire, or pursue other ventures. There were, however, a few Templars, including the 23rd and final Grand Master, Jacques de Molay, who refused to admit any guilt. Because of this, they were publicly burned alive at the stake in Paris on March 18th, 1314. Molay reportedly requested to be tied facing Notre Dame Cathedral and had his hands together in prayer when he was executed.[15] The funds and property of the Knights Templar were then transferred to the Knights Hospitaller of Saint John the Baptist. This Catholic military order exists to this very day. This is ironic as many false accusations against the Knights Templar involved John the Baptist. Before his execution, Molay publicly cursed those responsible for dissolving the Knights Templar. Pope Clement V and King Philip IV both died within a year.

Myths surrounding the Knights Templar have become incredibly popular in modern times. One of the legends is that Leonardo da Vinci is connected to them in some way. But the reality is that there is no true connection. It is unknown what his personal feelings about the Templars were. Whether he was in support, against, or indifferent to their existence remains a mystery. What we do know is that he was aware of them and had a decent understanding of the accusations against them. This includes how their belief in Saint John the Baptist was manipulated. Leonardo da Vinci was also aware of their ultimate demise as a military order. The main evidence that we have of this is because of da Vinci's love of Dante Alighieri's *Divine Comedy*, which directly calls out Pope Clement V, King Philip IV, and the Knights Templar.

14. Barber, *Trial of the Templars*, 185.

15. Martin, *Knights Templar: The History & Myths of the Legendary Military Order*, 125.

CHAPTER 5

Divine Comedy

FEW WORKS OF LITERATURE capture the human imagination so well that they are considered timeless. The ancient Greek story by Sophocles, *Oedipus Rex*, has moved across the centuries and inspired many pursuits in the fields of psychology and art. The Romans brought us great works as well such as the personal reflections of Marcus Aurelius in *Meditations*. William Shakespeare perfected love and reinvented the meaning of personal tragedy. The Russians gave us hope, despair, and personal responsibility. Jane Austen brought us social class and independence. And Ernest Hemingway gave us bravery, lust, alcohol, and love. The *Divine Comedy* by Dante Alighieri is another masterpiece that has remained just as valuable at the time it was written as it is in the present day. This long-form poem also provides literary storytelling compatible with the Catholic faith. Furthermore, it is a set of codes that scholars have been working on deciphering for centuries.

The *Divine Comedy* is an incredible poem that touches on the fundamental levels of artistic license and technical literary skill. The work has proven to be so influential that it is often referenced in the same regard as passages from the Bible are referenced. This poem is, of course, fictional in its nature as it is only a rendition of the afterlife. While on an artistic level, the *Divine Comedy* can supply great inspiration, it is not considered the Word of God. Dante skillfully applied his immense understanding of the Bible and applied that to this work. From there he quite freely decided to cast individuals he deemed unholy into his manufactured pits of Hell. It is an essential work regarding literature and the history of the Catholic faith. However, Dante has never been considered a prophet, and religious leaders do not attribute the *Divine Comedy* to having been delivered by God.

Dante Alighieri was an Italian poet and philosopher who lived from 1265 to 1321. Born in Florence, he went on to fight for the Guelph cavalry at the Battle of Campaldino in 1289. He wrote several works in addition to the *Divine Comedy*, including *Monarchy* in 1313. This piece of writing tackles the relationship of power between religious and secular institutions. It was later banned by the Catholic Church in 1585. Opting out of writing his works in Latin, Dante wrote in his native Italian thus making it the literary language of the West for centuries.[1] He further spent his time focusing on philosophical thought and produced additional literary works. He was eventually forced into exile for political reasons. It was during this time that he completed his most famous work, *Divine Comedy*.

This work is viewed as an allegory in the sense that each passage can contain multiple meanings. With this being the case, there have been many debates over its meaning throughout the centuries. Usually, when something like this occurs it is because the creator intends to cause bits of confusion. Therefore, it is just as likely that Dante did not have a specific reason behind certain lines, as he intentionally left them open to interpretation. What Dante has also done is leave a great deal of verses that have very specific purposes, many of which call out specific individuals. His directness, combined with a wealth of symbolism, is what truly makes this a masterpiece. Its influence is felt just as strongly today as it was when it was written.

Written approximately between 1308 and 1321, Dante's *Divine Comedy* paints a vision of the afterlife for both believers and non-believers. Never had a writer so eloquently depicted the Christian belief in an afterlife like what Dante had done. I also suspect that it may have been cathartic for him to cast his enemies into the fiery pits of Hell in his work. After all, this is literary fiction and was not meant to be taken literally. During the time that he was writing this work, the Knights Templar had been arrested and given a trial, and many were ultimately burned at the stake. Dante was keenly aware of what was going on with this and decided to add it to the *Divine Comedy*. King Philip IV is mentioned in the work as being financially greedy and unethical. Pope Clement V is also written about in the *Divine Comedy* as someone who is power-hungry and *lawless*. Also, the Knights Templar is given a spotlight as well by Dante having suggested in

---

1. Quinones, "Dante Alighieri—Biography, Poems, & Facts," line 9.

the work that they were disbanded so that King Philip IV could obtain their vast wealth.

John the Baptist is a central figure in the *Divine Comedy*. The prophet is referenced as the saint that replaced the pagan Mars as the overseer of Florence (Inf. XIII, 143–151.), and his image is set upon the currency of the people (Inf. XXX, 74.). A character residing in Purgatory also references Saint John the Baptist as a model for temperance (Purg. XXII, 151–154). Having historical knowledge of the Knights Templar and the reason behind their downfall creates a much clearer vision of what Dante was alluding to in the *Divine Comedy*. One example is the false accusation hurled at the Knights Templar that they denied the Sacrament of Baptism. This helps to tie in the religious importance of John the Baptist during the trials. Dante then further mentions John the Baptist throughout the work, illustrating his importance.

Centuries later, Leonardo da Vinci was fascinated by Dante's *Divine Comedy*. This epic poem was known throughout the West and prominently known throughout Florence. Renaissance artist and friend of Leonardo, Sandro Botticelli, illustrated 92 images of the *Divine Comedy*. Another contemporary of Leonardo, Michelangelo Buonarroti, created one of his most famous artworks, *Pietà*, from direct inspiration from the *Divine* Comedy.[2] Da Vinci himself even directly quoted and referenced the *Divine Comedy* throughout much of his material as well.[3] It even carried over into intellectual pursuits such as the *Paragone* which was a series of debates on various art forms. Giorgio Vasari, Bendetto Varchi, and Leonardo da Vinci are some of the noteworthy participants in these discussions. In the *Divine Comedy*, Dante questioned the use of painting, and da Vinci referenced those passages in his debates.[4] Therefore it is without question that da Vinci was not only aware of the *Divine Comedy* but that he knew it well enough to successfully incorporate it into his works.

The Renaissance was a time when wisdom was found by looking to the past. Ancient Greek and Roman traditions resonated with many people during the Renaissance. They contemplated what it meant to be alive, and how to progress civilization. It is easy to look at what is right in front of us

2. Paolucci, *Michelangelo: Le Pietà*, 13.

3. Museo Galileo, "Leonardo da Vinci and His Books: The Library of the Universal Genius," Line 9.

4. Museo Galileo, "Leonardo da Vinci and His Books: The Library of the Universal Genius," Line 11.

and disregard the historic movements that brought it there in the first place. But there is much to be gained from looking to the past for guidance. That isn't to say that one should wish to have lived in a bygone era, as nostalgic thinking can be poisonous if it saturates our minds. However, it is important to understand the concepts that figures in the past had learned. The thinkers of the Renaissance saw this in works such as the *Divine Comedy*. For them, it answered questions on both religion and literary merit, and they appreciated it for the artform that it was.

Pope Clement V, King Philip IV, and the Knights Templar are prominent characters in Dante's *Divine Comedy*, in which Leonardo da Vinci was well-versed. One example of how we know about da Vinci's sophisticated understanding of the work is that he regularly referenced it in his *Paragone* debates and personal notebooks. He also had a public quarrel with Michelangelo regarding the *Divine Comedy* in a piazza in Florence in the early 1500's. This means that Leonardo da Vinci was aware of the Knights Templar and the accusations of heresy connected to John the Baptist. Da Vinci's final painting, *Saint John the Baptist*, depicts the prophet as a healthy, youthful, and rebellious spirit. It is the first time John the Baptist had ever been depicted in this fashion in the history of Christendom. Here he is shown as a prophet brought between the crossroads of veneration, death, and the afterlife.

Leonardo da Vinci understood the importance of history and its stronghold on the present and the future. The Templars had been unjustly convicted for worshipping idols, abusing the Cross, and refuting elements directly relating to John the Baptist. The enormous influence that the Knights Templar had was expounded when Dante wrote about them and their aggressors in his famous work. Additionally, Dante mentioned John the Baptist several times throughout his legendary poem, further adding to his importance. Just as how the *Divine Comedy* draws in people from all backgrounds today, it equally held a grip on people during the Renaissance, including da Vinci. Leonardo da Vinci's link to John the Baptist precedes his own birth by several hundred years. The connection between them is much more than religiously based, he was da Vinci's inspiration.

CHAPTER 6

Florence Baptistery

LEONARDO DA VINCI LIVED his entire life surrounded by the influence of John the Baptist. A major prophet in the New Testament, it makes sense why he was a frequent figure, especially with the Vatican being nearby. John the Baptist is believed to have baptized Christ himself, in addition to being related to him. Factor that in with his brutal beheading, and you can have endless artistic interpretations. Da Vinci's contemporaries drew, painted, and sculpted John the Baptist. The prophet was also written about in Renaissance-era works, and he was prayed to at Mass. It is easy to see why da Vinci sketched and painted this holy figure many times. With the prophet being depicted regularly around him, da Vinci saw this as a challenge to paint him in a revolutionary way.

The city of Florence is considered by many to be the birthplace of the Renaissance. With the help of the notorious Medici Family, this intellectual and cultural *rebirth* paved the way for Florence to become a key city in world history. The philosophical and artistic flourishing that occurred here fed into other areas of Europe as well. During this time the town had also gone through several uprisings and shifts in power, all while maintaining influence and dominance. John the Baptist was also a main religious figure in the metropolis. The prophet was Florence's Patron Saint and was depicted on one of the sides of the Florin currency.[1] Many key figures, too

---

1. Berzock, "Caravans of Gold, Fragments in Time," line 1.

many to list, either spent time here or were born here. Florence was not only the nucleus of intellectual pursuits, but a place that provided endless inspiration.

Much of the Renaissance is because of the House of Medici. This powerful family funded many artistic and scientific experiments during this time. They understood that maintaining power was best done when cultural pursuits were at the forefront. The Medici family knew that a positive relationship with the public would bode well for them. Their rise to power began in the 14th century as they ran a robust banking system. This direct access to funds, along with strategic religious and political alliances, garnered them the title of royalty. Regardless of one's thoughts on the House of Medici, it is undeniable the amount of sway and respect they had. Their influence was strong throughout regions much farther than just that of Florence. This is why the Pazzi Conspiracy failed immensely. The Medicis had such strong support from the people they were essentially untouchable.

Between the Archbishop's Palace and the Florence Cathedral lies the Florence Baptistery. Also known as the Baptistery of Saint John the Baptist, this Catholic octagonal building has played an important role in Italian history. The date of its construction is unknown; however, it is believed to have been built somewhere between the 11th and 12th centuries.[2] Recent research suggests that the baptistery was being used as early as 1080, but construction carried on into the 12th century.[3] While the architect behind the building is also unknown, the octagon shape was common among other religious buildings. According to Timothy Verdon, a Roman Catholic priest and art historian specializing in sacred Christian art, the eight sides represent the extra day into the afterlife. In other words, Christians believe that God created the earth in seven days, and when the faithful depart they move to eternal life; the eighth day.[4]

The building is adorned with impeccable designs that have lasted throughout the centuries. On the exterior of the building is the symbol of the *Arte di Calimala* and the *Oculus of Scarsella* as a couple of examples. Inside the Florence Baptistery there are ornate decorations and designs fit for adoration. Leonardo da Vinci's teacher, Andrea del Verrocchio, created

2. Paolucci, *Il Battistero di San Giovanni a Firenze. The Baptistery of San Giovanni Florence (in Italian and English)*, 1.

3. Danziger, *Fiorenza Figlia di Roma: New Light on the Baptistery of San Giovanni and the Chronology of Florentine Romanesque Architecture*, 27.

4. Paolucci, *Battistero di San Giovanni a Firenze. The Baptistery of San Giovanni Florence (in Italian and English)*, 18.

the sculpture *Beheading of (John) the Baptist* in 1480 for the Baptistery. Da Vinci was in his late twenties when Verrocchio completed this sculpture. Another artist who created work for the Baptistery of Saint John the Baptist in Florence was his friend, Giovanni Francesco Rustici. He sculpted what is known as *Baptist Preaching*, a tryptic representation of Saint John the Baptist. The influence of John the Baptist was not only prevalent within Florentine culture for Leonardo but also with the people closest to him.

Giovanni Francesco Rustici (1474/1475–1554) was a painter and sculptor in the Italian Renaissance. According to Giorgio Vasari, Lorenzo de Medici placed Rustici as a pupil of Verrocchio's, the same teacher as Leonardo da Vinci. Vasari wrote about his friendship with Rustici and mentioned the ornate meals they shared. Rustici would have already been accustomed to luxury as he was born into nobility. During the Siege of Florence (1529–1530), Rustici fled to France and served King Francis I. But after the king's death, Rustici died destitute. King Francis I was the same king that Leonardo da Vinci went on to serve at the end of his life. Some mild evidence suggests that King Francis I was even at da Vinci's bedside at the time of his passing.

After Verrocchio left Florence for Venice, Rustici became a pupil of Leonardo's. Their friendship and artistic partnership flourished not only because of their connections to the Medici Family and Verrocchio but also because their fathers knew one another.[5] While sharing lodging, Rustici received a major commission from the Baptistery of Saint John the Baptist. He created the tryptic *Baptist Preaching* out of bronze and did this with the eager help of da Vinci. The influence of da Vinci on these sculptures is prevalent. Evidence suggests that the gestural composition of John the Baptist's hand pointing towards Heaven was later used for the da Vinci painting.[6] These works are recognized as some of the greatest artistic achievements of the Renaissance.

Florence operated as the generator of brilliance as the Renaissance looked to the past for inspiration. In modern times it can be fashionable to disregard history or outright condemn it. But what should always be remembered is that we are all products of our past, and there is much to be learned from it. John the Baptist was a major symbol throughout Florence and the Renaissance, and his influence was found in daily life. His impact is further reflected in the Baptistery of Saint John the Baptist. This

5. Morris, "Great Rustici Emerges from the Shadows," line 26.

6. Heydenreich, "Sculpture of Leonardo da Vinci," lines 36–41.

important holy site has strong ties to Leonardo da Vinci through the art-work of Giovanni Francesco Rustici. Another fact to note is that Dante Alighieri mentions this location in the *Divine Comedy* (Inf. XIX, 17, as an example). In Canto XIX, Dante writes about the eighth circle of Hell, which refers to the Baptistery of Saint John the Baptist, a building with eight sides. Furthermore, the Baptistery is where Dante himself was baptized.

CHAPTER 7

John the Baptist

SAINT JOHN THE BAPTIST is the last painting Leonardo da Vinci made during his lifetime. Over the years he created a string of masterpieces from *Lady with an Ermine* to *The Last Supper*. His painting of John the Baptist is no less a masterpiece. It is not only one of my favorite da Vinci paintings but is also one of my favorite paintings of all time. The inherent nature of the work simultaneously provides the viewer with realism and mystery. Despite there not being an official count, we know that the Roman Catholic Church recognizes more than 10,000 saints. John the Baptist is one of them. But even with such a high number of saints to choose from, Leonardo da Vinci continuously comes back to this one. For da Vinci, John the Baptist was a significant representation of the Crusades, the *Divine Comedy*, and the Florence Baptistery. It is because of this that the biblical life of John the Baptist needs to also be explored.

John is revered in many religions, including Christianity, Islam, the Bahá'í faith, the Druze faith, and Mandaeism. Many Christians believe that John the Baptist was prophesied in the Old Testament in Isaiah 40:3 which mentions a voice from the wilderness preparing for the Lord. There are many scholarly approaches to this verse, but the most straightforward explanation to it is that John is the one who baptized Jesus after living in the wilderness. In other words, he paved the way for Jesus to be viewed as the Messiah. Some academics believe that John was a part of the Essenes, a mystical Jewish sect that operated at the time.[1] One of the reasons behind this premise is that they also practiced baptism, which is what John is most known for.

Jesus and John being cousins stems from the traditional view that Jesus' mother, Mary, was related to John's mother, Elizabeth. Therefore, we know that they knew each other growing up, as Mary and Elizabeth were near one another in their lives. The reality is that John's birth is only mentioned in the book of Luke. However, there is no specific mention of them being cousins. Nevertheless, after the historic baptism, Jesus began his campaign to be known as the Messiah among the Jews. According to the New Testament, John the Baptist was later killed under orders of Herod Antipas after John chastised him for his divorce. The story of John the Baptist is mentioned in all four canonical gospels, as well as other Gnostic Gospels.

Tough questions remain regarding the story of John the Baptist. One of them being the nature of John's death. According to the traditional Gospels, Herod is tricked into beheading John by his new wife, Herodias. But another historian, Flavius Josephus (37–100), says John was killed after inciting mob violence by attracting a large, angry crowd against Herod.[2] Also, why did Jesus need to be baptized? Shouldn't it have been Jesus who baptized John? This question has stumped both scholars and religious leaders for many years. The truth is that there is no solid answer to this problem as only theories exist. One plausible theory is that Jesus may originally have been a follower of John the Baptist.[3]

Dr. Bart Ehrman is one of the most important living biblical scholars in the world. Religious leaders from low-level Christian pastors to high-ranking priests within the Vatican study under Dr. Ehrman to learn more about their faith. Often controversial, he brings his research to both his students and the public. This regularly puts him in the spotlight and creates backlash as it can be unsettling to the faithful. It should be said that he first started as an Evangelical Christian, but in recent years has described himself as an atheist. However, he is not the only leading biblical scholar who does not believe in God. Dr. Robert M. Price is a leading scholar in the New Testament. Not only is Dr. Price an atheist, but he publicly doubts that Jesus Christ even existed at all. So, in other words, if you want to study

---

1. Harris, *Understanding the Bible*, 382.

2. Schachterle, "Who Was John the Baptist? (The Untold Story)," lines 75–87.

3. Schachterle, "Who Was John the Baptist? (The Untold Story)," lines 33–37.

under the best researchers of the Christian Bible, it will be under atheists. The irony of these leading biblical scholars not believing in God is top tier.

Dr. Robert M. Price questioning the existence of Jesus is not that difficult to grasp once you start pulling back the curtain. While there may have been someone named Jesus with some type of following at the time, the only documentation we have are religious texts written decades later. No Roman records of his arrest or crucifixion, or anything else confirming his presence exist. The evidence, if you can call it that, is so dubious that we cannot be sure what this holy figure was like. There is a different type of Jesus you can read that depends on which canonical or non-canonical gospel you consume. Each *Jesus* has varying wants, needs, and desires. All of this is made to fit into the narrative of copious Christian sects.[4] I am not saying that Jesus did not exist, but I am also saying that there is no firm reason to think that he did either.

This concept of Jesus being more myth than reality is further cemented when you compare his story to other ancient ones that preceded him. The Egyptian god Horus and Greek god Perseus were conceived through divine interventions rather than intercourse. Dying and rising stories of deities are also found in the tales of Osiris, Adonis, and Dionysus. Miraculous healing and raising people from the dead are found in the ancient stories of Asclepius and others. The idea of being born as the Son of God is found in legends of Hercules, Krishna, and Romulus. A sacrificial death to save humanity and bring forth salvation is found in the stories of Odin and Attis. And descents into the underworld and then rising back up are also found in the myths of Ishtar, Orpheus, and Osiris. Each of these tales pre-date the existence of Christ by hundreds if not thousands of years. Religion and belief in deities are not as clear as the faithful would like. In addition to shared mythologies, many incongruities are found in the Bible.

In the book *Jesus, Interrupted*, Dr. Bart Ehrman discusses the many contradictions within the gospels. Regarding the baptism of Jesus Christ, he highlights variances that occur between the books of Matthew, Mark, Luke, and John. The first is that this baptism is not mentioned at all in the Book of John. The second is that the wording is significantly different between the books of Matthew, Mark, and Luke. In Matthew, the Heavens say, *this is my son, in whom I am well pleased.* This voice seems to be speaking either to Jesus or John the Baptist directly to inform them who Jesus is to be. But in Mark, the voice says, *you are my son, in whom I am well pleased.*

---

4. Price, *Deconstructing Jesus*, 17.

This variation is telling Jesus specifically who is. But in the Book of Luke, there is something different from the voice saying, *you are my son, today I have begotten you* which references Psalm 2:7.[5] The voice from the Book of Luke was quoted using older manuscripts of the Bible. This exact quotation is not found in modern, English versions.

These differences might seem like splitting hairs, but they actually created major confusion among early Christians. This is because each of those three gospels depicted major differences in the messaging. In Matthew, the voice identifies Jesus to John the Baptist and the crowd as the Messiah. In Mark, it confirms Jesus' identity to himself. And in Luke, the voice says that it was the baptism that made him God's son. These issues have not been resolved because they cannot be resolved. The differences are too large to mitigate. However, early Christians attempted to solve this problem by writing the Gospel of Ebionites that claims the voice came from Heaven at three separate times. Regardless, it still does not change the fact that the gospels mention three distinctly different things.[6]

In his book, *Heaven and Hell: A History of the Afterlife*, Dr. Bart Ehrman writes about the many misconceptions of the Christian view of Hell, often because of misinterpretations of the text.[7] These misconceptions are more than simply not understanding surrounding passages and its historical context. However, these major misconceptions often happen when religious thinkers do not consider the earliest copies of the Bible and its original language. Additionally, non-canonical writings by early Christians have helped play into the myth of Hell as being a place of eternal punishment. One of these concepts comes from the Apocalypse of Peter, which was written in the 2nd century. This text takes the stance that unbelievers are eternally tortured in Hell. The purpose of this was to scare people into believing that Christ was the Messiah.[8] However, the Apocalypse of Peter is not biblically backed, and no Christian denominations accept this text. Regardless, it is one of many ancient, unrecognized texts that ultimately played a role in our modern understanding of a Hell that eternally tortures those who do not believe in Jesus.

Dr. Bart Ehrman further points out other examples such as when Jesus mentions the fires of Hell. The direct translation for this is Gehenna,

---

5. Ehrman, *Jesus, Interrupted*, 39–40.

6. Ehrman, *Jesus, Interrupted*, 40.

7. Ehrman, *Heaven and Hell: A History of the Afterlife*, 1–2.

8. Ehrman, Heaven and Hell: A History of the Afterlife, 4–5.

a literal ancient trash heap in Jerusalem. In other words, he was referring to the fact that those who did not follow him would not receive a proper burial. This would have been a terrifying notion for ancient Jews. Jesus also never says the words *heaven* or *hell* at all in its original texts. Instead, he says words such as *Hades* and *Sheol* to describe an afterlife. Here we see the influence of the ancient Greeks and their thoughts on an afterlife.[9] Linguistical understanding is essential, especially when the ancient Hebrew word for *Sheol* is interchangeable with *pit* and *grave*. So, in other words, *Sheol* means death. It does not mean a place of existence after our earthly presence. There were movements roughly 200 years or so before the birth of Christ that questioned a mindfully present afterlife. However, there is no afterlife in Jewish tradition or theology. Once the world has closed over you, then you return to the dust in which you came.

The idea of an afterlife of a conscious, eternal punishment cannot be found anywhere in the Old or New Testament.[10] But the thought of an afterlife that rewards the faithful and eternally punishes heathens stirs an emotional response for believers. Christians believe in their eternal reward, and then unbelievers are violently attacked for the rest of time. This, tied in with early Christian lore, as well as misinterpretations from the original text, is why this thought persists. John the Baptist preached of the end times approaching. Two thousand years later we are still waiting. But he never talked about endless torture for those who did not have their sins washed away. Those who may have never heard of these original concepts of a Christian afterlife before should be aware that this is standard education in seminaries. Your priest or pastor was taught this in their doctoral education to become your religious leader. They are just choosing not to share this information with you.

Dr. Robert M. Price has done extensive research on John the Baptist and has discovered a great deal about the prophet. A point that Dr. Price likes to bring up is the high level of reverence that Jesus had for John. One of many examples of this is in Matthew 11:11 in which Jesus refers to John the Baptist as *risen* as well as there being no one *greater* than John the Baptist. This is one of many examples implying Jesus was a disciple of John the

9. Rosenthal, "Heaven and Hell': New history of the afterlife shows origins of the idea," lines 4–9.

10. Rosenthal, "Heaven and Hell': New history of the afterlife shows origins of the idea," lines 10–15.

Baptist before breaking off to lead his own religious movement.[11] Proposals such as this are obviously controversial. But again, these are standard subjects studied in the seminaries. After all, if you decided to devote your entire life to the writings in the Bible, wouldn't you want to understand it fully?

It may appear outlandish at the thought of Jesus being a follower of John the Baptist. However, evidence for this begins to stack up with another passage in the Bible, such as in John 1:15 and John 1:29–31. These passages have John the Baptist awkwardly state multiple times that Jesus had come before him. To ancient Christians this was wildly important because if John preceded Jesus in prophet-status then they run the risk of more followers flocking to John rather than to Christ. Remember, the canonical gospels state that John was already doing his popular ministry before Christ made his public appearance as the Messiah.[12] This wordplay contradicts its own gospels saying John was baptizing followers before Jesus' arrival. The Gospel of John is looking to quell any competition between Jesus and John in their respective congregations. Not to mention, as stated earlier in Matthew 11:11, Jesus had already referred to John the Baptist as *risen* and that no one is *greater* than him.

If you are still unconvinced with John the Baptist having his own following, you can look in the Book of Acts for proof. As written by Paul in Acts 19:1–7, he asked the people of Ephesus if they received the Holy Spirit. The people then said they were already baptized in the name of John. Paul then had them baptized again, but this time, in the name of Jesus Christ. Adding to this, the Pseudo-Clementine Recognitions talks about other disciples of John the Baptist who believed he, not Jesus, was the one, true Messiah.[13] An ancient individual with the power to baptize can lead to offshoots finding solace in him, rather than in Christ. This is further found in the Mandean faith, a religious group that still exists in the present day and believes John the Baptist as the final, most important prophet. As of 2025, there are estimated to be between 60,000 and 100,000 members of the faith. These numbers have continued to dwindle in the Middle East where they have little protection.

Matthew, Mark, Luke, and John are united in the front to dissuade anyone from becoming a follower of John the Baptist instead of Jesus Christ. So why include John the Baptist at all? My opinion is they had to include him.

11. Price, "Iron John the Baptist," lines 12–14.
12. Price, *Incredible Shrinking Son of Man: How Reliable is the Gospel Tradition?*, 115.
13. Schachterle, "Who Was John the Baptist? (The Untold Story)," lines 94–102.

John simply had too large of a following to be ignored. Therefore, if they incorporated him and attributed proclamations of John bending the knee to Christ, it would remove potential incentives for people to follow John. The writers of these canonical gospels further sweeten the deal by making Jesus the more desirable prophet to follow. They contrast Jesus and John by making John out to be the frail, hungry madman who wanders through the wilderness. I question this narrative as it would be challenging for someone like this to gain a large following by exhibiting those behaviors. The writers then depict Jesus in an almost opposite manner. Jesus turns water into wine, miraculously provides endless amounts of bread and fish, and even throws a huge dinner the night before his crucifixion. John the Baptist fasts, and Jesus Christ feasts.[14] Which party would you rather go to?

Another leading atheist biblical scholar is Francesca Stavrakopoulou, a professor at the University of Exeter. Her research has led her to believe that much of the stories in the Bible did not occur and that they are purely symbolic. Jordan Peterson, a psychiatrist and public personality, takes a similar stance to Stavrakopoulou. A distinction between these two is that Peterson believes the stories of the Bible, even if not historically accurate, serve a deeper purpose to humanity. While better symbolism can be found in reading Shakespeare and Fitzgerald, Peterson's idea of Christianity has become incredibly popular. We do not know how much of Christianity da Vinci believed to be true. However, Leonardo did not believe in the biblical flood story due to his study of seashells and fossils. He also openly questioned other aspects of the Bible throughout his adult life. Nevertheless, biblical figures, especially John the Baptist, influenced him profoundly.

Leonardo da Vinci's final painting of his life, *Saint John the Baptist*, features the prophet pointing upwards towards Heaven. His face is adorned with a subtle, yet confident smirk suggesting he may have already visited there. Or possibly maybe even just returned from there. But regardless of that interpretation, his posture and assured facial expressions tell the viewer he is confident about what the afterlife will bring. John the Baptist was an apocalyptic Jewish preacher who believed the end was near. Through the act of baptism, John preached that this cleansed believers and prepared them for an eternity with God. Many people voluntarily listened to and followed John the Baptist before Jesus Christ came onto the scene. He was a mighty figure with his own followers and also baptized the Christian Messiah.

14. Price, "Was Jesus (and) John the Baptist Raised from the Dead?," lines 41–46.

The story of John the Baptist left such an enduring impact that it can still be felt throughout the world. His influence not only helped to create the full picture of the Christian belief system but of other religions too. Furthermore, he led a powerful apocalyptic religious movement while alive, and then offshoots of other faiths developed based on their devotion to him. His name is plastered in schools, hospitals, cities, and so much more. Despite thousands of Catholic saints to have existed, Saint John the Baptist consistently appears to be one of the most popular. From the biblical stories to his influence during the Renaissance, we can see why Leonardo da Vinci developed a fascination with the prophet. Out of all the people that Leonardo da Vinci could have painted for the last artwork of his life, he chose John the Baptist. A revolutionary, sometimes controversial figure that cleansed the Son of God.

CHAPTER 8

Mythos

IN NOVEMBER 2023, I had the pleasure of lecturing at Yale University about Leonardo da Vinci. This event was put on in collaboration with student groups and the talk focused on the *Vitruvian Man* drawing. There are many layers to this drawing, one of them being that it was inspired by the ancient challenge of squaring the circle. This impossible task was a lifelong obsession of Leonardo's, and the *Vitruvian Man* searches for answers. Something interesting about this drawing is that it is comparable to a painting by Donato Bramante titled *Heraclitus and Democritus*, in which Leonardo da Vinci was used as a model. This painting was made around the same time as the *Vitruvian Man*. What we find when comparing these two works of art is something shocking: The *Vitruvian Man* is a self-portrait. The *Vitruvian Man* is da Vinci's self-portrait that places him in the middle of his obsession with squaring the circle. Pseudoacademics point to works such as the *Vitruvian Man* and make false claims that it is a hidden message relating to a secret, ancient organization. While this is an entertaining thought, it is purely fictional.

Some people have also claimed that da Vinci was a member of the Priory of Sion. This is inherently false as the Priory of Sion was created in the 1950's. Not only was Leonardo born hundreds of years before its founding, but the Priory of Sion was a major hoax. Another crazy one is that da Vinci was a member of the Illuminati, which is also not true. The Illuminati was founded in 1776, more than 250 years after the death of da Vinci. Even if the outlandish claims about a modern-day Illuminati are true, which they are not, Leonardo wasn't alive during its founding. The late intellectual, Christopher Hitchens, coined what is known as *Hitchen's Razor* which states *what can be asserted without evidence can also be dismissed without evidence.* In other words, whoever is the one making the claim is the one responsible for providing the evidence. If you have a theory about something, then prove it.

There are many reasons why it is difficult to piece together the life of Leonardo da Vinci. One reason is the little amount of firsthand documentation about Leonardo that was written when he was alive. In da Vinci's own notes, he tended to write backward, which makes deciphering some passages a challenging feat. Not to mention he wrote in an Old-World Italian, further complicating research. Leonardo also did not write much about himself in these notebooks either. Minimal firsthand accounts exist that deal specifically with da Vinci, and this only adds to the legends built around him. It is much more difficult to attribute fables to historical figures that have been well documented. Pseudo-research makes headway when dealing with historical figures in which little is known about their personal life. The greater the man, the greater the legend.

Starting with da Vinci writing backward. This was not to keep his notes a secret from onlookers as the explanation is much more simplistic. He was left-handed. Writing from left to right meant that his palm would have smeared the ink as he wrote. So instead, he developed a system of writing backgrounds to prevent this issue from occurring. After all, writing backward could only prevent someone walking by from seeing what he was writing. But if someone were to have stolen his notebooks then the backwards handwriting would only have been a mild hindrance. We also do not see any evidence in these notebooks that da Vinci deemed them classified. He was much more preoccupied with his inventions than he was with someone stealing his work. Backward handwriting adds to the mystique of Leonardo da Vinci, but it was only out of utility.

Claims have been made about da Vinci being a vegetarian but there is limited source material to substantiate this. He may have preferred not to eat meat. However, this was not a realistic way to stay nourished in the Renaissance. Another ridiculous claim is that Leonardo left secret codes in his paintings. This is easily disproven by asking a simple question: How could someone leave a hidden code in a painting that could only be deciphered by modern technology? Furthermore, every painting that da Vinci made has been extensively x-rayed, and not one of these scans has shown any hidden messages. Many false claims about Leonardo da Vinci have been attributed to him. However, it is essential to remember that evidence is needed for these assertions.

Art historian, Stephen Campbell, has warned that researchers have been motivated by presumption rather than by evidence regarding Leonardo.[1] This fill-in-the-blank approach to this historical figure dilutes who he really was, and makes accurate research more difficult. Scientific processes were far from being established, so da Vinci relied on his curiosity for his inventions. He looked at the natural world around him for inspiration and for how things could operate. His insights came to him from his observations, not from what we deem now to be scholarly approaches.[2] This doesn't mean that da Vinci would have rejected modern approaches to scholarship. It just means that these approaches simply did not exist at the time.

Da Vinci's understanding of anatomy helped to dictate the figures that he painted and drew. Artistic merit was a top priority, and depicting anatomical features correctly came second. This, however, does not mean that it wasn't important. For example, da Vinci's painting *Saint Jerome in the Wilderness* (1480–1490) shows remarkable anatomical accuracy. This is especially seen in the figure's neck and collarbone. As for the *Saint John the Baptist* painting, the figure is of perfect proportions. Even Saint John's hair falls with gravity in a precise manner. Researchers have published scholarly articles that say Leonardo depicted the aortic arch, and other aspects of the heart, in the *Saint John the Baptist* painting.[3]

Leonardo da Vinci was a great man, but no more than a man. He wasn't a god or a demi-god. He wasn't a prophet or an oracle. Rather he was an incredibly intelligent and curious man who set out to do great things. While secret societies and confidential religious orders existed during the Renaissance, Leonardo was not a member. If on the small chance he was, we do not have any evidence to support it. Da Vinci was interested in his work, which included a great number of inventions for use in combat. This is yet another piece of evidence that contradicts a false claim about him. Many people like to fashion Leonardo as a pacifist. The truth is that he spent much of his time inventing weaponry. It is true that later in life he

1. Huls, "Uncovering the Myths of Leonardo," lines 9–13.

2. Brinkhof, "Ken Burns on what we get wrong about Leonardo da Vinci," lines 10–12.

3. Keshelava, "Hidden Cardiovascular Anatomy in "Saint John the Baptist" by Leonardo da Vinci," lines 4–6.

expressed reservations about warfare, however, this is a far cry from him being an outright anti-war activist. Many strange claims have been made about da Vinci, and I am sure more is to come. However, it is imperative to remember that every claim requires solid evidence.

Gavin Menzies was a British submarine lieutenant-commander and author. He wrote several successful books including *1421: The Year China Discovered America* and *The Lost Empire of Atlantis: History's Greatest Mystery Revealed*. Unfortunately for Menzies, virtually none of his theories are factual. The notion of ancient Chinese fleets discovering North America has never been proven by any other researcher. Even Chinese scholars do not agree with his assessments. As far as believing he discovered Atlantis, well, there is no evidence for that either. The overtly romanticized hunt for this underwater city has been popular since Plato wrote about it in *Timaeus* and *Critias*. Modern scholarship makes clear that these writings from Plato were meant as an allegory and not to be taken as fact. Menzies also made incorrect claims about Leonardo da Vinci and his inventions in another book.

In his book *1434: The Year a Magnificent Chinese Fleet Sailed to Italy and Ignited the Renaissance*, Gavin Menzies claimed that the Chinese brought intellectual information to Europe in 1434 which set off the Renaissance. One of his claims is that they brought over the *Nong Shu*, the Chinese Book of Agriculture originally written in 1313 and that the Europeans copied it. He even claims that da Vinci copied from it and wrote it down in his notebooks. The problem with this assertion is that there is no evidence behind it. Most, if not all, of da Vinci's pages in his notebooks can be found online and in print. You can cross-examine these documents for yourself, and you will see there is no correlation. Menzies cross-referenced similarities between the *Nong Shu* and Renaissance documentation. However, these comparisons are barely similar to each other. There is also not a single Renaissance replica of the *Nong Shu* or any other bit of evidence showing that a Renaissance document was inspired by it.

Menzies did not approach his theory with the necessary academic rigor that is required. Instead, he relied on a storyline that was quick to grab attention and then rode the wave of hoping his readership did not question his lack of evidence. Scholars reviewed what he claimed were copies and unanimously decided that no such material was ever made. They even go on to say that some of his examples only carry mild similarities. But there are no copies, and only occasionally mild similarities.[4] He did

4. Castle, "Columbus debunker sets sights on Leonardo da Vinci," lines 55–63.

not seem to understand the documents he was reviewing either. One of his claims is that Leonardo copied his flying helicopter design from the Chinese.[5] Da Vinci's helicopter drawing is even featured on the front cover of his book. The issue with this claim is that what da Vinci drew was not a helicopter. It was a theatrical prop designed to assist actors playing angels to float down from the sky. It was never supposed to fly but rather meant to spiral downward.[6]

It is common for people to fill in the blanks with things they don't know the answer to. They will even do so with unfounded personal theories. A garbage answer for them is better than no answer at all. The subject of conspiracies is fascinating because they sometimes turn out to be true, or partially true. But often they are nothing other than fiction. If a bold claim is made by someone, the first thing that I ask myself is, *how does this person know this information, and I do not?* That simple question tends to diffuse any sway that person may have had. There are many falsehoods attributed to Leonardo da Vinci and much of this comes from people wanting to know more than what they do. But a deeper reason for this is that they want to feel safe and in control. If they believed da Vinci knew the secrets of the universe, then at least someone out there was made aware.

---

5. Menzies, *1434: The Year a Chinese Fleet Sailed to Italy and Ignited the Renaissance*, 166–176.

6. Isaacson, *Leonardo da Vinci*, 45.

CHAPTER 9

Investigative Reporting

BEFORE DAPHNE CARUANA GALIZIA'S assassination from a car bomb in 2017, she made a career out of investigative reporting. Naturally, she had many enemies, and threats to her family became a regular part of their lives. Before Galizia was killed, her assets had been frozen because of the many libel cases pending against her. The freezing of her funds had been approved by Malta's economy minister. Furthermore, the previous death threats and arson attacks on her home have all gone unsolved.[1] It is fair to say that Galizia was an agitator and some of her reporting ultimately led nowhere. Other reports of hers may have even carried more opinion than fact, however, this is common for a journalist. You would be pressed to find any reporter who had never gotten a story wrong. But Daphne Galizia did get many stories right, and she paid the ultimate price for it.

The infamous Panama Papers made the news in 2016. This shocking revelation leaked more than eleven million original documents that detailed a variety of illegal transactions. This included financial information regarding wealthy citizens as well as public officials.[2] When this story broke it was almost a wet dream for the infantile *eat the rich* brats that loathe anyone who has made a success of themselves. What these people

1. Attwood, "year after her murder, where is the justice for Daphne Caruana Galizia?" lines 19–24.

2. ICIJ, "new ICIJ investigation exposes a rogue offshore industry," lines 16–19.

later realized was that much of the Panama Papers only showed how these wealthy people shuffled their money around. Ultimately it wasn't that interesting of a story which is why shortly after the Panama Papers were released everyone seemed to have forgotten about it. There was, however, some noteworthy information that came out. One of them was that 13,000 shell companies had been registered in Samoa.[3] In 2019, several years after the Panama Papers were published, a total of $1.2 billion dollars had been recovered via back taxes, fines, and litigation.[4]

In 2016 on Galizia's blog *Running Commentary*, she reported that the government minister of Malta, Konrad Mizzi, had questionable connections in New Zealand. From this same reporting Galizia suggested that she may have a network of spies that provide her with this type of information.[5] The plot thickens when Galizia reported a few days later that Keith Schembri, the Chief of Staff to the Prime Minister of Malta, owned a comparable trust also in New Zealand. This trust was then connected to a Panama company.[6] Galizia's breaking of this story thrusted her even more into the spotlight. But from there she didn't stop her investigation. In 2017, she alleged that Michelle Muscat, Maltese Prime Minister Joseph Muscat's wife, owned a questionable company in Panama as well.[7] Daphne Galizia was assassinated later that year.

In November 2019, Prime Minister Joseph Muscat said he was considering a pardon for the supposed middleman in Galizia's murder. The following day, Maltese businessman Yorgen Fenech was arrested on his yacht for a possible connection the assassination.[8] Fenech is the owner of 17 Black, a mysterious Dubai-based company. Daphne Galizia had written about this company in her investigative reporting and published it in the Panama Papers. Her reporting reveals connections to high-profile individuals, such as Keith Schembri and Konrad Mizzi.[9] Arrests and protests in Malta soon followed. It must be said that Daphne Galizia's reporting is

3. AP, "Panama Papers: The South Pacific's role," lines 4–5.

4. Dalby, "Panama Papers helps recover more than $1.2 billion around the world—ICIJ," lines 1–3.

5. Galizia, "Konrad Mizzi's and Sai Mizzi Liang's Easter lunch," lines 1–5.

6. Xuereb, "Konrad Mizzi has no regrets over acquisition of company in Panama; PM's chief also has Panama company, say reports," lines 1–12.

7. Ganado, "Daphne Caruana Galizia. . . Malta's most controversial journalist," lines 14–15.

8. BBC, "Malta businessman held on yacht in journalist murder probe," lines 1–6.

9. BBC, "Malta Caruana murder: Resignations spark government crisis," lines 1–27.

her own work and what is being relayed here has come from her and other journalists. I am not taking any specific stand on who may or may not be guilty or implicated in Galizia's assassination.

Daphne Galizia gained a sizeable following when she was alive. She wrote for various publications and her blog *Running Commentary*, which anyone today can still access, was wildly popular. Galizia's feuds had no limits either. In April 2014, she wrote about Maltese politician, Dr. Emanuel Mallia's Easter card by writing, *That fat, tawdry hypocrite with a mail-order bride 30 years his junior, a stash of wealth made from working for criminals, murderers and cocaine-dealers, and the fabled generosity of a Pharisee, has sent Holy Joe Easter cards to all his constituents.*[10] Galizia was an agitator and singlehandedly rocked the country of Malta with her investigative reporting. But her petty feuds could be one of the reasons she was denied government protection. It is an excellent example of testing the boundaries of free speech. She left a profound impact, but her trivial jabs in some of her reporting seem to have created unnecessary enemies.

Daphne Galizia not only had a wide readership but seems to have had sources around the globe. Many of them have not been identified, but much of the information they provided has been substantiated by other reports. Questions remain about their identities. How many of them were moles of her journalistic targets? Did she know her sources by name? Could she have been betrayed by a source? A whirlwind of thoughts can be created by going down this rabbit hole. The truth is that we may never know who these people are or were. What is also not publicly available is whether she had a personal system of cross-checking her sources. However, her network seems to have been reliable enough that other journalists rarely countered her discoveries. But what we do know is that her journalistic reach went far beyond the borders of the tiny island nation of Malta. Nowhere was off limits for Daphne Galizia.

Galizia also wrote more than just what was reported in the Panama Papers and personal grievances she had with Maltese politicians. Her range of topics was wide and included writing about the Knights Hospitaller of Saint John the Baptist. The history of these Knights has a lasting influence in Malta and many of their citizens have a strong connection to them. Because of this, Galizia shared a story in 2009 about the discovery of an underground

---

10. Galizia, "New meaning to painted tombs—with this one, even the exterior fails to impress," lines 1–2.

tunnel system connected to the Knights.[11] As critical as she was about Malta, her love for the nation and its history ran deep. Galizia also reported on religious groups within the country. A notable example of this was her public spats with the controversial Catholic group, Opus Dei.[12] While the Knights Hospitaller has historical roots in Malta, both the Knights Hospitaller and Opus Dei have a strong influence in its modern society.

The people of Malta are suspicious of their government and any perceived secretive organization. Much of this can be viewed in the social media accounts of Maltese citizens and Malta's mainstream news organizations. Daphne Galizia was one of these people weary of these perceived secret groups. In addition to writing about the Knights Hospitaller and Opus Dei, she wrote critically about Freemasons. One of her attacks against them came only one month before her assassination.[13] Daphne's paranoia about secret societies had increased up to the time of her death. Much of her reporting was coherent and well-researched. However, she later in life must have known that a major attack against her was coming. She just didn't know where it would come from. Shortly after her death, then Prime Minister Joseph Muscat shared a new Smashing Pumpkins song titled, "Knights of Malta" on X. The Knights of Malta was originally called the Knights Hospitaller of Saint John the Baptist. His post received significant backlash from people who were more concerned about his alleged connection to Daphne's assassination, rather than for the song.

11. Galizia, "From National Geographic News," line 1.

12. Asciak, "Daphne's Article is three years late," lines 1–10.

13. Galizia, "So many Freemasons cluttered around Delia," lines 1–15.

CHAPTER 10

The Plague

THE BLACK DEATH (1346–1353) stemmed from the Bubonic Plague and was one of the deadliest pandemics in history that killed somewhere between 25 and 50 million people. Those fortunate enough to have survived were left with little more than hopelessness and despair. It is thought by modern scientists that the Black Death spread rapidly through the air and also latched onto fleas. The bacterium Yersinia pestis is believed to be the culprit.[1] The devastation brought on by the Black Death led to many types of religious, political, and cultural upheavals. This pandemic was so severe that it is still remembered and discussed. However, for someone like Leonardo da Vinci, born in 1452, the memories of generational trauma were still fresh. As for da Vinci's painting *Saint John the Baptist*, it is an artwork that promises salvation and solace for the faithful from devastating events such as this.

There is still much to be debated regarding the origins of the Black Death. However, there is a consensus that the bacterium Yersinia pestis was already around for thousands of years and that various sanitation factors led to its rise. The Black Death is estimated to have killed off roughly 30% to 60% of the European population, as well as around 33% of the population in the Middle East.[2] It took hundreds of years for Europe to regain its

---

1. Haensch, "Distinct clones of Yersinia pestis caused the black death," lines 3–5.

2. Aberth, *From the Brink of the Apocalypse: Confronting Famine, War, Plague and Death in the Later Middle Ages*, 9–13.

population levels. Unfortunately, with the Black Death having occurred so long ago, modern science struggles to gather helpful evidence to discover how exactly it came about. A prominent theory is that fleas from dried grasslands in Asia latched onto rodents arriving in Europe.[3] As much as scientists have uncovered about the Black Death, much of its origins and how it spread remain a mystery.

In addition to the massive death toll, the Black Death exposed the vulnerabilities of medieval society. Problems with sanitation, minimal healthcare, and lack of germ theory contributed to the disease's rampage. Socially, it pushed along changes in Europe such as with the feudal system and social mobility. There was also an increase in skepticism regarding the Catholic Church and religion. When tens of millions of people are dying around you, it becomes harder and harder to think of it as being God's will. Trauma is an overused word today, but regarding what happened during the Black Death it does not seem like a strong enough word. For years to come, it would be depicted in art and literature and regularly referenced in other cultural areas. The Black Death left a profound impact on the collective society of Europe. It is a permanent reminder of how fragile our lives are.

Among the paintings, drawings, and inventions of Leonardo da Vinci, we see many allusions to death. His mural *The Last Supper* covers the holy meal before the torture and killing of Jesus Christ. Da Vinci's painting *Saint John the Baptist* features the prophet pointing upwards towards the heavens and the afterlife. His military inventions, such as more efficient crossbows and catapults, show an obvious use for eliminating enemies in battle. His 1479 drawing of the hanging of Baroncelli after taking part in the Pazzi Conspiracy illustrates death by execution. It is impossible to ignore da Vinci's curious nature, even when dealing with the subject of dying. There is also the large number of cadavers that da Vinci secretly operated on. His obsession with how the body functioned, as well as its lifeless state was extensively written about in his notebooks. Leonardo seemed to have been quite comfortable with the notion of death.

The Black Death was one instance of the Bubonic Plague. Over the years there had been several other breakouts of the Bubonic Plague, and da Vinci survived one of them. While residing in Milan, a series of plagues from 1484–1485 swept through the city and killed around 50,000 people.[4]

3. Tignor, *Worlds Together, Worlds Apart, Volume 1: Beginnings to the 15th Century*, 407.

4. Liddell, "Plague that Inspired da Vinci to Design a City. We Should Steal His Idea," lines 1–3.

He was one of the lucky ones to have survived the onslaught. Da Vinci never wrote about this in his notebooks and his close contemporaries never wrote about his thoughts on it either. Because of this, it is hard to know what his mental state from surviving it was like at the time. He was someone who was fascinated with how the human body functioned. However, his curiosity for this seemed to only be in controlled manners, like studying cadavers in a hospital-type setting. So, with possible impending death, it is difficult to know how he approached this. What we do know is that after the plague left Milan, he immediately drew up plans for a new city.

Milan was a narrow, crowded, dirty city when da Vinci lived there. With a major lack of germ theory, it was not known how germs contributed to the plague. It does seem that da Vinci still understood that cities needed open spaces with a focus on sanitation.[5] His dreamed-up city had wide roads and was built on several levels.[6] This sense of urgency that da Vinci had with drawing up plans for a new town also stresses the significance of the plague. Despite Leonardo's extensive, well-thought-out idea, it was never implemented. Demolishing a major city and building up a new one with multiple stories was certainly out of the budget. Leonardo's intelligence and imagination were regularly on another level.

Even if Leonardo da Vinci's city were to have come to fruition, it would only have quenched the need for physical safety. In the primary sources we have, especially when paired with his religious art, da Vinci was a Catholic. The thought of the afterlife constantly weighed on him, and under the Christian faith, the only way to the Father is through Jesus Christ. According to Christians, one of the necessary ways to help achieve this is through baptism. This is the heart of why John the Baptist carries such affection among the faithful. He is the one who baptized the Son of God in the holy Jordan River. A spacious, multi-level city may prevent a future plague from ravaging Milan, but it is baptism that provides the faithful with an everlasting life.

Da Vinci lived through a time of intense turmoil and witnessed the vast changes that swept across Europe because of the plague. In addition to the death that it brought, it also disrupted social life. Europe was forever changed. The Milanese Bubonic Plague of 1484 to 1485 lasted no more than 18 months, but within this short period, it destroyed tens of thousands of

---

5. Liddell, "Plague that Inspired da Vinci to Design a City. We Should Steal His Idea," lines 7–13.

6. Melis, "Leonardo da Vinci designed an ideal city that was centuries ahead of its time," lines 37–45.

lives. From what we know, Leonardo da Vinci never contracted the sickness but was instead stuck with its psychological effects. Experiencing something as damaging as this left a profound influence on his later works. His fascination with the human body was only compounded by the plague as he ramped up his anatomical studies after its devastation. His exploration of death as shown in his art and notebooks also increases after this period in his life. How our bodies live and how they later die enraptured his mind. *Saint John the Baptist*, the last painting he ever created, further highlights this fascination.

CHAPTER 11

Knights of Malta

THE KNIGHTS HOSPITALLER OF Saint John the Baptist constructed many important buildings, several of which still exist. A great deal of these structures were churches and hospitals located in the towns that Leonardo da Vinci resided in. One of these buildings includes the Hospital of San Sepolcro at the Ponte Vecchio in Florence. Once operated by the Knights Templar, the Knights Hospitaller of Saint John the Baptist took it over following their dismantling. Another example in Florence is the Hospital of Santa Maria Nuova.[1] This hospital is the oldest, still active hospital in Florence. It is also the hospital that Leonardo da Vinci is famous for operating on human corpses for his anatomical studies. The influence of the Knights Hospitaller of Saint John the Baptist was strong, which further inspired Leonardo da Vinci.

When the Kingdom of Jerusalem fell in 1291, many Crusaders, including the Knights Hospitallers, were relegated to smaller areas of control. To regain control and land, the Knights Hospitallers took over the city of Rhodes in 1310, located in modern-day Greece, after four years of war. Immediately after their takeover of Rhodes, they managed to gain control over neighboring islands as well, such as Kastellorizo. While these successful conquests were occurring, Pope Clement V and King Philip IV forcefully dismantled the Knights Templars. Much of the Templar's remaining funds

---

1. Hume, *Medical Work of the Knights Hospitallers of Saint John of Jerusalem*, 457–458.

and properties were transferred over to the Knights Hospitallers, increasing their power. Once established in Rhodes, some people began referring to them as the Knights of Rhodes.[2]

The Knights Hospitallers were called many different names over the years. Technically, most of these names are considered official. However, it can become confusing as this list has grown quite long. But it is vital to remember that even as their namesake changes, they are still the same Catholic military order, originally known as the Order of Knights of the Hospital of Saint John the Baptist of Jerusalem. Their naming structure has changed plenty over the years, but their organization has remained the same. After claiming Rhodes and its surrounding islands, over the next several decades they faced increasing attacks and attempted invasions against their strongholds. By the 15th century, many of the attacks they faced were from Ottoman pirates. However, these attacks were only petty when compared to what was about to come.

In 1522, Sultan Suleiman the Magnificent of the Ottoman Empire launched around 100,000 soldiers at the Knights, who only had roughly 7,000 fighting-age men at the time.[3] The battles lasted around 6 months, but with the Knights Hospitallers not making progress and suffering heavy losses, they retreated to Sicily. Philippe Villiers de L'Isle-Adam, the Knights Hospitallers 44th Grand Master, was their leader at the time. Despite losing in the conflict, both sides still viewed him as a brave, noble leader. Pope Adrian VI regarded him as a defender of the Catholic faith. But the removal of the Knights Hospitallers from their strongholds was anything but the end for them. In many ways, it was only the beginning. What these warrior monks were about to do would make them a permanent fixture for the years to come.

Seven years after their removal from Rhodes, they were given Malta. This was done through negotiations between Pope Clement VII, who was also a member of the Knights Hospitaller, and various kingdoms. Beginning in 1530, they took this land as their own for the next 268 years. There was some tension between the Knights and the local Maltese people. These issues mainly stemmed from the locals initially being banned from joining the knighthood, as well as from the Knights sleeping with the local women.[4] However, the Knights Hospitallers were overall seen as a favorable

2. Herbermann, *Hospitallers of St. John of Jerusalem: Catholic Encyclopedia (1913)*, 3.

3. Balfour, *Ottoman Centuries: The Rise and Fall of the Turkish Empire*, 176.

4. Sugden, *Nelson: The Sword of Albion*, 122.

group. Some notable reasons for their successful coexistence were that they boosted the economy, provided charity, and protected them from Muslim invaders.[5] With the established presence of the Knights Hospitallers in Malta, they were then affectionately referred to as the Knights of Malta.

The Knights Hospitaller, now known as the Knights of Malta, began building hospitals, fortresses, watchtowers, and churches. This rapidly transformed this tiny island of simple means into a mighty stronghold. Hospital expansions in Malta not only provided services to more of its sick citizens but also brought in updated technology. Several hundred years later the Knights of Malta helped establish the nation's first public library, in 1761. A few years later in 1786, the country's first university was founded, also with the help of the knighthood. Malta still has strong ties to these Knights. These ties are not just because some pope placed them there hundreds of years ago, or even because of their innovation and charitable work. What ties the Knights of Malta to the country of Malta is their devotion to the nation. The Knights of Malta protected and served the island, and the island reciprocated this act.

Existentialism did set in with the Knights of Malta in a similar fashion to what happened to the Knights Templar. When the Templars began losing ground, their military operations stalled, and the purpose of their existence came into question. The same happened to the Knights of Malta. This Catholic military order was used for battles and conquests and fighting for the Holy Land. Now they were left to care for a tiny island in the Mediterranean. The Knights took their military prowess and original objective of the Crusades and started protecting Christian sailors in the Levant. This came to be known as the *Corso*.[6] Despite operating on less funding than they were used to, they now had a greater sense of purpose. Their patrolling of the Mediterranean led to many of them raiding and plundering Muslim ships. These attacks, however, were beyond the set expectations.[7]

With the Knights of Malta living lavishly from their plunder, they were operating under an increasingly unstable Roman Catholic Church. Protestantism was becoming more popular, and religious attitudes were shifting. Many Knights joined various navies to serve a specific nation. This led people to worry that this would increase the likelihood of members of the Knights of Malta fighting each other on behalf of a country. The historic

5. Prata, *Angels in Iron*, 10–11.

6. Earle, *Corsairs of Malta and Barbary*, 97.

7. Earle, *Corsairs of Malta and Barbary*, 109.

unity of this order began to wane. Then in 1789, the French National Assembly abolished the Knights of Malta and their sovereignty in France.[8] This did not destroy the Knights of Malta, but it diminished their influence. The real harm came to them when Napoleon Bonaparte captured Malta in 1798. Marking the end of the Knights of Malta's control of the island, the Knights were dispersed and no longer had land to rule over.

Even though the Knights of Malta no longer had land to govern, they still had the Vatican on their side. Many resources had been poured into them over hundreds of years, and they weren't about to dissolve into oblivion. They not only acquired great skill sets but were united by an ancient history. Out of all they had accomplished in Malta and the surrounding regions, they remained a knighthood. Originally known as the Order of Knights of the Hospital of Saint John the Baptist of Jerusalem, they now went by the Knights of Malta, with a foundational devotion to Saint John the Baptist. Historically, the Knights of Malta have killed, and they have been killed. Their history of blood and charity was not going away because they no longer carried authority over a small island.

The Knights of Malta has never been destroyed. Despite all that has happened to them, their knighthood remains. Other contemporary groups, such as the modern-day Knights Templar, have no connection at all to the original Knights Templar of the Crusades. However, the Knights of Malta today have a direct line to the Knights of the Christian Crusades. Today the Knights of Malta are an incredibly influential group, not only in religious life but also in the highest echelons of society and politics. From 2000 to 2013, Israeli archeologists excavated a site in the Christian Quarter of Jerusalem. They uncovered the Hospital of Saint John the Baptist, founded by the Knights of Malta around the 1100's. This hospital could care for upwards of 2,000 people and cared for patients of all religious backgrounds. They also accommodated the Jewish people by providing Kosher foods. In addition, it operated as an orphanage.[9] The Knights of Malta's influence was strong back then, just as it is strong in the present day.

8. Robinson, *Decree Abolishing the Feudal System*, 404–409.

9. Mairav, "Mideast's Largest Crusader-Era Hospital Unveiled," lines 17–29.

CHAPTER 12

Provenance and Restoration

EPIPHANIUS OF SALAMIS (310–320—403) wrote critically about a prominent Christian sect known as the Borborites. This ancient Christian group has no surviving texts to provide us with firsthand accounts regarding their particular practices and beliefs. All historians have to go off of is the writings of Epiphanius, a staunch enemy of the movement. Because of this, it is also hard to date this group's existence. Most scholars view the group as having existed from the 2nd century and lasted until the 6th century. The Borborites' sacred scriptures incorporated many Gnostic Gospels, including at least four devoted to Mary Magdalene.[1] Additionally, they included the writings of what is now considered to be parts of the New Testament. Remember, this group existed long before the Bible was first translated and compiled into a single book in 405. This means that they were pulling from multiple sources for their religious devotion. The notion of a unified group of early Christians sharing a consistent belief about Jesus is far from accurate; in reality, different groups held varying views of him.[2] The Borborites were one of them.

So why did theologians such as Theodoret of Cyrus (393–458) and Saint Epiphanius of Salamis think disparagingly of them? It is because the Borborites had unconventional views of the sacred texts and their meaning.

---

1. Kim, *Epiphanius of Cyprus: Imagining an Orthodox World*, 37–39.
2. Price, *Deconstructing Jesus*, 265.

A major variant among this group compared to others at the time is that they were an ancient Christian sex cult. They were far from being an outlier regarding this too. Another early Christian group that performed ritualistic sex acts was the Carpocratians, who were founded in the 2nd century. The Borborites, Carpocratians, and other similar groups were devout believers in Jesus Christ and the biblically accepted books. They also had additional holy texts that covered different topics, such as the various Gnostic Gospels centered on Mary Magdalene. It can be easy in modern times to see the outlandish nature of a Christian sex cult. However, what needs to be remembered is that these groups operated long before the compilation of what is now known as the Christian Bible. These groups of Christians believed that they were following the true, authentic teachings of Christ.

According to Epiphanius of Salamis, in the Borborite Gnostic Gospel titled *Greater Questions of Mary*, we are given a disturbing interaction between Jesus and Mary Magdalene. According to Epiphanius' telling of this Gnostic Gospel, Jesus brings Mary Magdalene to the top of a mountain where he proceeds to pull a woman out of his side and have sex with her. Jesus then consumed his own semen at which Mary Magdalene fainted at the grotesque sight. Upon waking, Jesus reminded her to keep her faith strong. Epiphanius then says that Borborites not only consumed semen but also menstrual blood. He further suggested that this is their origin story for consuming the body and blood of Jesus Christ. In other words, the Borborite's ritualistic sex acts were a way of partaking in the Eucharist and Holy Communion.[3]

As previously mentioned, none of the Borborite's Gnostic Gospels exist in the present day. The only information that we have comes from their adversaries. Many modern scholars doubt the authenticity of what was supposedly written in these lost gospels because adversaries had every incentive to belittle the Borborites. That being said, it is a fact that ancient Christian sex cults existed and that they were rooted in a deep love and devotion to Jesus Christ. What also matters is that the legend of the Borborites and their lost Gnostic Gospels have lived on. So just as we do not have all of the answers to Leonardo da Vinci's final painting, *Saint John the Baptist*, we have enough information to put together an understanding of it. The same rings true for these ancient Christian groups like the Borborites. We may

---

3. Ehrman, *Peter, Paul, and Mary Magdalene: The Followers of Jesus in History and Legend*, 234–235.

not know every detail about them, but we know enough for a base-level understanding of their religious motivations.

Another area to call out is that sexual desire for holy Christian figures did not begin with da Vinci's painting, *Saint John the Baptist*. As in many early Gnostic Gospels, the concept of physical attraction runs rampant. So, while da Vinci's painting of John the Baptist was revolutionary for its time, he was not the first person to depict a Christian prophet as a sex symbol. Early Christians wrestled with many competing concepts in the 350 years or so after the death of Christ. Much of it was not settled until the year 405 with the first unified translation and compilation of the Old and New Testament. But even after 405, many Christians had a difficult time disregarding the Gnostic Gospels. During da Vinci's lifetime, mainstream Christian viewpoints were largely settled. One of them was that John the Baptist was always to be depicted as a gaunt, frail figure that wandered through the wilderness. That was until da Vinci decided to depict the prophet as a sex symbol, ushering in a sensual innuendo in a similar fashion as the Borborites.

Saint John the Baptist has always been an influential figure as the notion of baptizing the Messiah carries inspirational effects. Leonardo da Vinci grew up in a time and region that was particularly inspired by him. Just as it is today among Christians, belief in John the Baptist during the Renaissance was of the highest importance. Because of this, it is no surprise that da Vinci depicted John many times throughout his life. Some examples of this include the *Angelo Incarnato*, *Virgin of the Rocks*, and *The Virgin and Child with Saint Anne and Saint John the Baptist*. This list is not exhaustive. There are also works potentially made by Leonardo that feature him as well. An example of this is *Bacchus* which the da Vinci scholar, Martin Kemp, believes may have started as a painting of the saint.[4]

My connection to the *Saint John the Baptist* painting runs deep on a personal level. In 2022 I had the great pleasure of being an official art Copyist for the Louvre Museum in Paris. Copyists have a long tradition at the Louvre dating back to the French Revolution where they paint a copy of a work of art inside the museum. Their tenure generally lasts upwards of three months. Thousands of artists from around the world apply and few are selected. It is estimated that only 150–250 artists a year are granted the coveted permit to paint inside this museum. I was given this high honor and humbling experience of painting my own renditions of the *Mona Lisa* and *Saint John the Baptist* by da Vinci inside the Louvre. I have not been

4. Kemp, *Leonardo*, 251.

able to escape this saint, just as Leonardo, as well as historical and modern society, hasn't been able to either.

This captivating painting embodies the humanist ideals of the Renaissance while simultaneously paying reverence to the religious figure. John represents spiritual purification and repentance and builds a bridge between the Old and New Testaments. Leonardo portrays the Baptist as a youthful, vibrant, and androgynous person. This likely harkens to Leonardo's religious conviction and confidence in the afterlife. The enigmatic smile is reminiscent of the *Mona Lisa* which further connects these masterpieces. Leonardo was aging rapidly at the time he painted it. But by placing a similar grin on John, he communicates to the viewer that he is at his apogée. The Baptist was a mystical precursor for Jesus and da Vinci effortlessly captures this. The influence of John the Baptist throughout da Vinci's life culminated in this moment.

The date of completion for the *Saint John the Baptist* is disputed. However, the common understanding is that the painting was made from 1513 to 1516. Some scholars suggest that Leonardo did not finish it until 1517. Regardless of the differences in dating, it is universally accepted that this was his final painting. He died shortly after its completion in the year 1519. Only some of da Vinci's paintings were in his possession when he died which includes the *Mona Lisa* and *Saint John the Baptist*. These two works are part of a very small list of paintings that we are certain that Leonardo painted. Authorship of other disputed works by Leonardo da Vinci is complicated. It takes a wide variety of evidence to come into place to form an attribution. Some strategies utilized include x-rays, visual opinions from scholars, and provenance of the artwork if there is one.

Provenance, which is the history of ownership, is helpful in verifying artwork. Unfortunately, the record keeping of artworks in the Renaissance was far from a streamlined process. No system is perfect but tracing an artwork's history carries value as it can help prove that an artist made a specific work. Documentation matters. As for the *Saint John the Baptist* painting, knowing that Leonardo died with it in his possession is a helpful starting point. It was believed to have been in the collection of French King Francis I at Fontainebleau in 1542. Later, King Louis XIII of France gave it to King Charles I of England in exchange for a painting by Titian and Hans Holbein in 1625.[5] The painting was then sold to the banker, Eberhard Jabach, in 1649. For a time, it was owned by Cardinal Jules Mazarin. Then in 1661 it

---

5. Zöllner, *Leonardo da Vinci: The Complete Paintings*, 248.

went back to France and was owned by King Louis XIV. After the French Revolution it entered the permanent collection of the Louvre.[6] Having this detailed provenance for a da Vinci painting is extraordinary.

A vital component in the art world is provenance. Not only does it serve as a record of chronology, but it helps to assert authenticity, value, and cultural significance. Clear provenance provides transparency as to the history of the artwork. Without it, we would see even more art forgeries than we already do today. Another imperative aspect regarding provenance is that it adds a much-needed context to not only the artist's oeuvre but also to historical events. As interest from private collectors and museums purchasing works continues to grow, the need for accurate provenances will grow as well. The *Saint John the Baptist* has a solid provenance. Additionally, in recent years it has also undergone a vital restoration.

Art restoration is a delicate and oftentimes contentious issue. Some argue that it is necessary to both preserve the artwork and to have it present itself as the artist originally intended. Others have argued that it runs the risk of being overly restored, and removes the nuances made by the artist. Both sides are true. We must be prudent with restoring art, and it should be done with great care. Old paintings of the Renaissance in existence today only contain about 30% to 50% of their original paint. The rest have been filled in by art restorers. If restoration is deemed necessary, then it must be approached with caution and restraint. A common need to restore old paintings is that they tend to have many layers of varnish on top of them. This varnish fogs the painting and can change its color. But even then, the varnish needs to be removed thoughtfully.

There have been many scandals over the years from botched restorations, so when it is suggested, there is typically an outcry. After having last gone through a restoration in 1802, the *Saint John the Baptist* was due for another one in 2016. The main reason for this is that it had turned to an orange hue. The culprit was seventeen layers of varnish added to the artwork over the years. The French Museum Center of Research and Restoration is located in the basement of the Louvre. They are known as the C2RMF team. Through their use of X-rays and other available technologies, they were able to look deep into its layers of paint. This gave the restorers a strong sense of how to approach the painting's restoration and to see these layers of varnish.[7] After the successful 2016 restoration, viewers are now able to

6. Zöllner, *Leonardo da Vinci: The Complete Paintings*, 248.
7. Tarbox, "Risky Business of Restoring Leonardos," lines 10–53.

see this painting in the way Leonardo meant for it to be seen. Dark shadows hugging the body of John the Baptist, a thin reed cross, and a mysterious smile. This painting is a portal to another form of existence.

CHAPTER 13

The Louvre

THE GOSPEL OF THE Nazarenes is a non-canonical gospel that is not a part of the traditional Christian Bible. Much debate has arisen from this text but there are a couple of indisputable facts regarding it. The first one is that it is not a modern forgery. Extensive research has been performed, and it is universally accepted as authentic. The second is that while we do not know its exact dating, we do know it was written sometime before 200 AD. One of the main reasons why we know this is because there is substantial documentation that Clement of Alexandria, a theologian and philosopher, studied and referenced it before 200 AD. In the Gospel of the Nazarenes (sometimes referred to as the Gospel of the Hebrews), Jesus was urged by his mother and brothers to be baptized by John the Baptist, which Jesus initially refused. Upon reflection, Jesus decided to be baptized by John (Jerome, quoting "The Gospel According to the Hebrews" in Dialogue Against Pelagius III:2).

While the Gospel of the Nazarenes came about more than 1,250 years before the birth of da Vinci, we do not have evidence that suggests he was aware of this text. Nevertheless, it is an incredible piece of writing that provides enormous insight in the history of early Christianity. One of these reasons is because John the Baptist is further seen as an incredibly powerful figure. So powerful, in fact, that Christ's mother and brothers urged Jesus to be cleansed by him. It is ancient stories such as this that add to the allure of John the Baptist. Additionally, Leonardo da Vinci's final painting of his life,

Saint John the Baptist, adds a great deal of mystery to our understanding of this prophet. Ancient holy texts, such as the Gospel of the Nazarenes, provide unique insight into John the Baptist. This is similar to how Leonardo's artistic renditions of the prophet provide us with unique visuals as to how he interpreted him. Leonardo's painting, *Saint John the Baptist*, currently resides in the most famous museum in the world.

If you pay attention, you will notice the intricate details carved into the outside walls of the Louvre as well as the many sculptures attached to it. The courtyard is busy during the day, especially during the warmer months. But once the sun sets and the day becomes night, few people are seen walking around. It is there, late at night, where you feel like the Louvre belongs to you. It is quiet and the architecture glows with beauty and mystery. The lights that shine on the museum give off a golden hue, making it seem like an ancient, lost palace only recently discovered. It reflects our past while remaining steady towards the future.

The *Rose Line* may sound like a fantasy out of Dan Brown's book, *The Da Vinci Code*. While the book is fiction, it has inspired many conspiracy theories because the *Rose Line* is based on the real Paris Meridian. This line runs directly through the heart of Paris and rivals the famous Greenwich Meridian in London. The Paris Meridian also had useful functions for it as well because it served various measurements. One of these measurements was to find the figure of the Earth via the arc measurement method. In 1994, Dutch artist, Jan Dibbets, was commissioned to create well over 100 medallions to go along the Paris Meridian. These bronze coins display the name *Arago*, after the French mathematician, François Arago. One of these medallions is in the outdoor courtyard at the Louvre. On a trip to Paris, it took my wife, Erin, and I a little while to locate it. Erin ended up finding the medallion after it was essentially right under our feet. It is worth noting that François Arago was a high-ranking Freemason which has further added to conspiracies regarding the Paris Meridian.

Resting on the bank of the Seine River in the 1st arrondissement, the Louvre was originally a fort designed to protect Paris from foreign invaders. Built in the 12th century under King Philip II, the original medieval structures can still be visited in the museum's crypt. Some historians speculate that the initial structure is even older than the 12th century. Nevertheless, over the years the Louvre has served several purposes and undergone many renovations. Over time the Louvre began collecting more works of art and many public proposals asked to display the collection. It was under the last king of France, Louis XVI, that made the shift for the Louvre to become a royal museum.[1] After the French Revolution, the Louvre was then made into a public museum. From here there were many changes made in an administrative context. However, the royal pulse of the museum remained.

This museum holds well over 600,000 objects in its permanent collection and sees around eight million visitors annually.[2] The line to enter the museum through the massive glass pyramid begins early. However, the ticket check is relatively seamless, and the visitors scatter once inside. Everyone does pour in to see the *Mona Lisa*. My advice is to get tickets for the Louvre on a weekday and go early. Once you enter the museum make your way to see the *Mona Lisa*. The room fills up quickly so once you have that out of the way then you can enjoy the rest of the museum to your liking. The *Mona Lisa* is a true masterpiece. It is one of the greatest, if not the greatest artwork of all time. It is not to be missed. Something amusing that I regularly hear is that people think the *Mona Lisa* is small. However, this famous painting is a standard portrait size for the time of the Renaissance.

Many mysteries remain about the Louvre. This vast palace has its history in a time when record keeping was not common practice, leaving historians to fill in the blanks. Additionally, there are lesser-known facts about the Louvre as well. King Louis XIV is known for moving his royal court from the Louvre to the Palace of Versailles in 1682. What most people do not know is that this meant that the Louvre was left virtually empty for many years. During this time, artists squatted in its empty halls.[3] Another interesting, but not well-known fact about the museum is that you can view the original 13th century moat excavated by archeologists. This can be seen below the Cour Carré under the glass pyramid.[4] The list seems to be endless of what can be discovered in this museum.

The Louvre Museum is more than a popular destination, it is a cultural and historic institution that plays a vital role in caring for the treasures of the world. Its collection spans from ancient civilizations up to the modern day. This offers a unique window into the history of both creative minds and humanity itself. This museum's commitment to education, research, and conservation ensures that we can have a clear understanding of these

---

1. Carbonell, *Carbonell Museum Studies: An Anthology of Contexts*, 56.

2. Cheshire, "Louvre retains its place as the most-visited art museum in the world," lines 5–14.

3. Blumenthal, "13 Things You Didn't Know About the Louvre," lines 51–59.

4. Itzkowitz, "10 Secrets of the Louvre, The World's Most Visited Museum," lines 19–22.

objects and their place in history. The Louvre continues to inspire new generations of thinkers and artists because it embodies culture and art. By visiting the Louvre, people experience the significance of its collection because it builds a bridge to broader cultural contexts that shaped humanity. The Louvre is one of the most important locations on earth.

CHAPTER 14

Shipwreck Island

THE REPUBLIC OF MALTA is a tiny European nation that pulls in surrounding traditions that form its own culture. With warm waters and a bright sun, it makes for a popular vacation destination. Another aspect is that trade happens with relative ease with critical shipping routes moving through the seas in the region. Italy rests to the north of this island, and we can see this inspiration saturate their land. Libya and Tunisia are the other countries closest to Malta and its influence is also felt. From the Greeks and Romans to the Knights Hospitaller and Napoleon Bonaparte, the history of rule in Malta is vast. It is a small country with a small population; however, it is influential to the rest of the world. Therefore, just as placing the *Saint John the Baptist* painting within its proper historical context is essential, the same must be done for Daphne Galizia in Malta.

Paul the Apostle was born around the same time as Jesus Christ and went on to persecute the early Christians in Jerusalem. We know that it was a violent persecution, but do not know the specifics of it. The Apostle Paul never went into detail on how he attacked them and there are no other documents detailing this either. He does say that he destroyed their gatherings and hauled the early Christians away to prison. It is unlikely that Paul had access to take them to prison and we know this for several reasons. The first one is that we do not have any historical, or biblical, descriptions of Jewish prisons in the time of Jesus and Paul. Additionally, the Roman authorities would never have imprisoned people because an obscure Jewish sect demanded so. Historians have substantial documentation from this period, including of prisons, and there are no mentions of Jewish ones, or Romans obliging these requests. Therefore, the way he attacked and imprisoned them is unknowable.[1] Nevertheless, Paul had a religious conversion on the road to Damascus and became a follower of Christ.

The Apostle Paul then devoted his life to spreading the message of Jesus Christ throughout the Mediterranean basin. During his travels, he wrote important commands for Christian believers, including for them to spread the news of Jesus as the Messiah. Paul's intense style of evangelism and preaching led to him being arrested by Roman authorities and was to sail to Rome for trial. During their voyage, Paul and the Romans shipwrecked on the island of Malta. Paul surviving the shipwreck is an adventure story for Christians. It is also viewed by many believers as God protecting Paul so he could continue evangelizing. Paul was later executed, likely through beheading, because of spreading the new message from God. The parallels between the Apostle Paul and John the Baptist line up in an interesting way. Both died via beheading under orders from a powerful leader after proselytizing their faith. They also evangelized in the sense that the only way to Heaven was through spiritual purification.

In present-day Malta, the citizens take pride in their historic ties to the Apostle Paul. An important biblical figure having roots in your nation after surviving a shipwreck instills a sense of honor. While Malta does have freedom of religion, its official state religion is Catholicism. As of 2024, almost 90% of their citizens are Christian, with nearly all of them being Catholic.[2] Religion is an important backdrop in Malta as many of their ancient churches are still in use to this day. The Knights of Malta have a strong presence in the nation and their influence is felt throughout the island. There are also several other religious organizations such as Opus Dei that operate there. However, with the country constantly facing allegations of corruption, conspiratorial attitudes towards them are prevalent.

By 2018, Malta was one of the fastest growing economies in the European Union. But as it rose in the ranks, corruption grew with it. The assassination of Daphne Galizia in 2017 and the events that followed are hands down the nation's biggest scandals. However, many other factors of corruption, unrelated to Galizia, have occurred. A scheme of selling Maltese

1. Ehrman, "How Paul Persecuted the Christians," lines 1–9.

2. Borg, "90% Caucasian, 83% Roman Catholic: Malta census statistics released," lines 1–20.

citizenship, which includes a legitimate passport, for $1 million made its citizens weary due to known corruption within its political ranks. Buyers of the citizenship included Russian, Nigerian, Saudi Arabian, and Chinese tycoons. Allegations suggest this allows foreign nationals to move freely through the European Union without other nations knowing their true origins. Since 2020, Malta has made around $1 billion dollars from this.[3] Making citizenship available for purchase isn't necessarily scandalous. But there have been accusations of politicians receiving financial kickbacks from the program. Malta's population is only around half a million people, which magnifies its corruption. This nation also has a history of being a haven for pirates, so these roots run deep.[4]

This quaint island in the Mediterranean boasts a rich history and a blend of cultures. Today, Malta is a thriving, high-income economy, with tourism playing a significant role in its prosperity. The country's strategic location has made it an attractive destination for travelers and businesses. Malta's capital, Valletta, is the smallest capital city in the European Union but is incredibly beautiful as it sits right on the coastline. A 2021 census stated that the entire nation of Malta has a population of only 542,000 people. Valletta alone only has a population of around 6,000 people as of 2025. The country's stunning architecture, beautiful beaches, and vibrant culture make it an ideal destination for tourists. An entire nation with a population of a small American city can easily make someone stick out, especially if they are investigative journalists.

In recent years, Malta has become a hub for financial services, online gambling, and blockchain technology. This may or may not be contributing to the corruption that plagues the nation. The country offers a favorable business environment, a skilled workforce, and membership in the European Union, thus making it an attractive location for foreign investment. Despite it being an economic powerhouse, the low population levels tend to not put them on the cover of world news. But when German manufacturing sinks or there are stalls in imports and exports in France, it is what we first see on our phone's news alerts. But Malta being a tax haven for unchecked organizations goes relatively unnoticed. Malta is a unique and fascinating country that blends its rich history with modern innovation. But despite being a member of the European Union, some of their politicians act as if they have free range to do whatever they please.

3. Wertheim, "Inside the corruption allegations plaguing Malta," lines 41–63.
4. Wertheim, "Inside the corruption allegations plaguing Malta," lines 32–33.

In 2006, Malta decided to display the Maltese cross on their new Euro. The design was between two images with the other of Jesus being baptized by John the Baptist. A strong polling majority rejected Jesus and John the Baptist being shown on their currency. This rejection was not because of disdain for the prophets, but because of their reverence for them. They did not see it fit to have religious figures displayed on money.[5] Catholicism is heavily intertwined in Malta. The biblical story of the Apostle Paul surviving a shipwreck off the Maltese coastline to the Knights of Malta still operating there shows a strong Christian influence. The Feast of Saint John the Baptist is also a popular celebration in the country. This is held every year on June 24th and is hosted by the Knights of Malta. Guests include ambassadors, politicians, and celebrities. John the Baptist was a major influence everywhere Leonardo da Vinci went in his lifetime. Additionally, this same holy prophet has an everlasting presence on this tiny island that rests in the Mediterranean.

5. Grech, "Maltese cross most popular by far," lines 1–36.

CHAPTER 15

The Renaissance

WITHIN THE REIGN OF the Renaissance was what is known today as the High Renaissance. This brief period lasted only a couple of decades yet left a profound impact on the world. The whole of the Renaissance was a renewal of ancient ideas while simultaneously reaching towards the future. But it was during the High Renaissance specifically that marked a moment dominated by the giants: Michelangelo, Raphael, and da Vinci. Most of what the Renaissance is known for is because of what occurred during these years. It came on as fast as a lightning bolt and vanished just as quickly. Leonardo da Vinci did his best work during this time, which includes his painting, *Saint John the Baptist*. The entire duration of the Renaissance brought about many great moments as Europe was digging itself out of its Medieval period. But it was the High Renaissance where things truly met their peak.

The High Renaissance began around 1490 and ended in 1520 after the death of Raphael. Some historians have argued that the High Renaissance lasted until the Sack of Rome in 1527. However, the 1520 date is commonly referenced because there was a noticeable shift in artistic styles after Raphael passed. The shift occurred because artists felt restricted by repeatedly painting the same images, like cherubs. They needed more. Mannerism was the next movement that took over around the year 1520. This period focused on style over realism by using techniques of exaggerated anatomy and flamboyant colors. Artistic freedom during Mannerism was built from the strength of the High Renaissance and is visible in the art that was produced. Movements in artistic style are constantly changing, and this depends on a wide range of factors, many of which are cultural. Placing art into only two camps of *realism* and *abstraction* misses the point entirely of what artists are trying to achieve. Artists are constantly looking for innovation and pushing their limits.

Michelangelo di Lodovico Buonarroti Simoni, known simply as Michelangelo, created incredible work during this time. A sculpture of his that has been extensively studied by academia is his *Pietà*. This artwork shows Mother Mary holding a perished Jesus Christ across her lap. Art historians believe this sculpture references a passage in Dante's *Divine Comedy, O virgin mother, daughter of your Son. . . your merit so ennobled human nature that its divine Creator did not hesitate to become its creature* (Par. XXXIII, 1–6).[1] With the body of Christ sprawled out across his mother's lap, we see the anguish and possibly even some resentment from Mother Mary. She is shown holding his body almost as if he was still an infant. Reflecting on the few short decades she had with her son; she knew that this ultimately would be his fate. Christian theology believes Mother Mary gave birth to more than a prophet. She was the mother to the Son of God.

The psychology of this sculpture runs deep as well. *Hansel and Gretel* is a German fairytale published in 1812 by the Brothers Grimm. Symbolically, this is a story of the psychological theory of the *devouring mother*. This is regularly discussed by the psychologist, Jordan Peterson. In the story, the children are lured by a witch into a home that has everything they could ever want as children: candy. But ultimately this childish desire provided by the witch ultimately destroys them. The *devouring mother* theory states that mothers who infantilize their children destroy them more than anything out in the world ever could. An overprotective mother with high levels of trait-neuroticism can cripple their children in psychological ways so that they will never be able to participate in life successfully as adults. Michelangelo's *Pietà* shows the other side of this as it runs the risk of your child being hurt by the world. The only catch is that being hurt by the world is not nearly as terrible as being demolished by a mother.

Raffaello Sanzio da Urbino, popularly known as Raphael, is another titan of the High Renaissance. Raphael's artwork differed from Michelangelo and da Vinci in several ways. Michelangelo tended to focus more on 3-dimensional muscular highlights. Leonardo focused on lines so soft that you could barely, if at all, tell that they were there. Raphael preferred

1. Paolucci, *Michelangelo, la Pietà*, 9.

a geometrical balance across the image while focusing on human relation-ships. His 1518–1519 painting, *La Fornarina*, has intrigued art historians for centuries. This woman is depicted with an idealized beauty. Her breasts are exposed with a falling top and a soft smile to engage the onlooker. Much is unknown about the subject. Some believe her to have been a romantic companion of Raphael's, some believe her to have been a prostitute, some think she was a baker's daughter, and others think she was a witch.[2] Regard-less, the painting is a masterpiece. Raphael left such a strong mark on the High Renaissance that his passing marked the end of the entire movement.

The High Renaissance was not only a time of creating memorable art. There were also earthquake-like shifts in the political and religious land-scapes. Girolamo Savonarola was a Catholic leader who fought strongly against corruption with the clergy. Born in 1452, the same year as da Vinci, he amassed such a large following that he effectively replaced the Medici Family and took power in Florence. Setting out to turn Florence into the *New Jerusalem*, he laid out a hardline Christian doctrine that was to be fol-lowed by every citizen.[3] Savonarola rose to power in 1494, but his govern-ing ended in 1498 after his outspoken criticism of the Catholic Church. He was hanged and burned at the stake in Florence but remained a Catholic to his very last day. Regardless, when the Protestant Reformation began less than 20 years after his execution, Martin Luther regularly cited Girolamo Savonarola as a precursor to the movement. Girolamo Savonarola's short reign left a lasting impact. He is viewed by historians as being the *John the Baptist* of the High Renaissance.[4]

Leonardo da Vinci certainly was aware of who Savonarola was be-cause he went back to live in Florence in 1500. It is not known to the extent to which da Vinci supported Savonarola. What we do know is that he was asked to review a document from Florence that most likely was written by either Savonarola or one of his close associates. He may have even met him in person regarding the creation of the Sala del Maggior Consiglio.[5] Ar-guably the most famous portrait of Girolamo Savonarola was done by the artist Fra Bartolomeo. This artist not only knew Leonardo da Vinci but was very much influenced by da Vinci's style.[6] Fra Bartolomeo created many

2. Segal, *Painted Ladies: Models of the Great Artists*, 39.

3. Weinstein, *Savonarola: The Rise and Fall of a Renaissance Prophet*, 122.

4. Farley, "Girolamo Savonarola, The Prophet of Florence," lines 1–4.

5. Acidini, "Palazzo Vecchio, Sala dei Gigli," lines 23–26.

6. Britannica Editors, "Fra Bartolommeo," lines 4–5.

works depicting John the Baptist. One of his most notable paintings is *The Rest on the Flight into Egypt with Saint John the Baptist* from around the year 1509. This painting features both Jesus and John the Baptist as infants.

Despite Fra Bartolomeo's prolific career as an artist, he ceased creating art for several years after becoming a being a follower of Girolamo Savonarola. Savonarola demanded many changes to Florentine culture and the arts fell under this umbrella. Bartolomeo picked up his brushes again in 1504, several years after Savonarola's hanging. Many other artists abandoned their work because of Girolamo Savonarola's influence. One of the reasons for this is that these artists tended to be Catholic. So, if the ruling Catholic authority proclaimed art to be blasphemous, then it was better to stop painting than to offend their God. Much of this came to a head in 1497 with what is known as the *Bonfire of the Vanities*. With the support of Savonarola, thousands of objects were burned that included mirrors, books, art, and any other object that could be deemed as a vanity.

Sandro Botticelli, a close friend and collaborator of Leonardo da Vinci, was also a follower of Savonarola. While there have been claims that Botticelli participated in the *Bonfire of the Vanities* and burned his artwork, there is not enough evidence to support this. Botticelli did create a painting around 1501 titled *The Mystical Nativity*. This painting is based on a Christmas Eve sermon that Girolamo Savonarola gave in 1493. His words in this sermon included:

> *Behold, the sky opened, and right away I see descending from the bosom of the Eternal Father a venerable woman with an olive branch in hand, and she came singing, Misericordia Domini plena est terra. That is, the earth of the Holy Virgin was filled with the mercy of the Lord. She urged and begged the Child to come forth, and thus, Veritas de terra orta est. Suddenly from this 'earth' was born Truth. The Holy Child came forth. Then he set himself on the bare ground in front of the Holy Virgin. Now as soon as this Truth had come forth, Mercy met with her, and the two embraced each other and said, Universe vie Domini misericordia et veritas: All the ways of the Lord are mercy and truth. And while these things were being done on earth, Iustitia de celo prospexit: Righteousness looked from the sky. And seeing this marriage of the Son of God with human nature, and wishing to come to that banquet, she took leave of God and descended forthwith to earth, shouting and singing, Gloria in excelsis Deo. And lo, from the other part of heaven came a woman in a simple, white, and pure dress who was most beautiful and graceful, and with great haste she ran towards Righteousness, and they kissed*

each other; and thus, Iustitia et pax obsculate sunt. And forthwith one of them, who was Lady Peace, said, Et in terra pax hominibus bone voluntatis. And so all four met together and united forever, so that anyone who might have one of them should have them all.

This is almost identical to Botticelli's painting. Savonarola received inspiration for this sermon from Psalm 85:10–11 which reads as *Love and faithfulness meet together; righteousness and peace kiss each other. Faithfulness springs forth from the earth, and righteousness looks down from heaven.*[7] The passage from the Book of Psalms as well as the Christmas Eve speech made the inspiration for one of Botticelli's greatest paintings. The influence from the few years that Savonarola reigned lasted well beyond his death and can be seen in *The Mystical Nativity* painting. Throughout his career, Botticelli also made many depictions of John the Baptist such as the *Virgin and Child with Saint John the Baptist* painted around the year 1500. Sandro Botticelli and Fra Bartolomeo are just two examples of artists swept away by the sermons of Girolamo Savonarola.

During this tumultuous time, Leonardo moved back to Florence, known as his Second Florentine Period, in 1500. He moved into a monastery under invitation from Servite monks called the Santissima Annunziata. This monastery still stands tall to this day. Inside the building are beautiful works of art on the high walls and ceilings. Several depictions of Saint John the Baptist are painted inside this monastery too. Leonardo da Vinci saw these images at every turn while living there. From Savonarola being compared to Saint John, and associates of da Vinci following Savonarola and creating paintings featuring John the Baptist adds to this influence. Furthermore, da Vinci is now living in a monastery that has images of John the Baptist on the very walls that shelter him.

Artist, Alessio Baldovinetti, painted *The Baptism of Christ* for the Santissima Annunziata roughly 50 years before da Vinci moved there.[8] It is one of only a few surviving works by Baldovinetti. This scene follows standard rules for depicting Christ being baptized. One of these rules require Jesus standing in shallow water while John baptizes him by pouring water on his head. Around 25 years after the Baldovinetti version, a young Leonardo assisted his teacher, Andrea del Verrocchio, with their own version titled *The Baptism of Christ*. This version followed a similar structure to Baldovinetti. Da Vinci worked on several parts of this painting,

7. Hatfield, "Botticelli's Mystic Nativity, Savonarola and the Millennium," lines 1–44.
8. Britannica Editors, "Alessio Baldovinetti," lines 13–18.

including the ripples in the water and the angel featured on the far left. The small painting by Baldovinetti was attached to two other paintings of his, *The Last Supper* and *The Ascension*, to create a panel. *The Last Supper* by Alessio Baldovinetti has several similarities to da Vinci's version as well. One notable aspect is that the seating is structured in a way that the biblical figures are looking outwards at you. Alessio Baldovinetti also went on to create a mosaic on the doors of the Florence Baptistery.[9]

Around the time da Vinci was living at the Santissima Annunziata, he painted *The Virgin and Child with Saint Anne*. This painting depicts Mother Mary, Saint Anne, and Christ as an infant with his hands on a lamb. The symbolism shows that Jesus is the Lamb of God. But da Vinci also makes an interesting perspective of dynamics here by not only having Mary sitting on Anne's lap, but Anne is proportionally much larger in height and scale than Mary. This playful composition baffles da Vinci scholars to this day. Around the time da Vinci started this painting, he made the largest drawing of his life titled, *The Virgin and Child with Saint Anne and Saint John the Baptist*. Also known as the *Burlington House Cartoon*, this drawing made with black and white chalk was done on 8 separate sheets of paper that were glued together. Its exact measurements are 55.7 inches by 41.2 inches. The largest drawing da Vinci ever made featured a depiction of John the Baptist. This drawing inspired other artists such as da Vinci's student, Bernardino Luini, in his 1530 painting, *Holy Family with Saint Anne and the infant John the Baptist*.

One of the reasons why John the Baptist was such a popular figure during the Renaissance is due in part to a biography that Dominican Friar, Domenico Cavalca, wrote about the prophet.[10] Cavalca lived from 1270 to 1342 and was a major influence not only during his life, but for hundreds of years after he had already passed. His impact was felt in his biography of John the Baptist because it was a fictionalized account of the prophet's childhood. The reason for doing this was because we do not have any writings in the Bible of John the Baptist's upbringing. This became a central document to many artists of the Renaissance as a source of inspiration. It is also why there were so many depictions of John the Baptist as an infant during this time. Domenico Cavalca also wrote, while claiming to cite Saint

9. Britannica Editors, "Alessio Baldovinetti," lines 27–28.

10. The National Gallery, *Episode 4 | Infancy | Saint John the Baptist: From Birth to Beheading | National Gallery, London*, 0:52.

Jerome, that Mary Magdalene was betrothed to a prophet named John.[11] It is unclear whether Cavalca was referencing John the Baptist or not. However, it does highlight one of the many examples that people pondered the thought of Mary Magdalene having been married.

It is peculiar that Domenico Cavalca cited Saint Jerome when writing that Mary Magdalene was betrothed to a prophet named John. Cavalca having died in 1342 means that he lived many hundreds of years after the death of Christ. However, Saint Jerome was born between 342 and 347 and died in 420. So, while Saint Jerome still lived a few hundred years after the crucifixion, his timeline is significantly closer to it than what Cavalca was. In case you forgot, Saint Jerome is the person responsible for creating the Vulgate. This was the first compilation and translation in a unified language of the Old and New Testament in the year 405. There is, however, no existing documentation that Saint Jerome ever wrote this. All we have is Cavalca's writing, which claims Saint Jerome had written this. But what matters isn't necessarily whether the claim came from Saint Jerome or not. What matters is the myth and legends that transpired from it. Concepts of a holy union have entranced people for thousands of years because of folktales like this.

The High Renaissance was a thunderous moment in history where the whole of the Renaissance exploded within a couple of decades. Amazing art was created not only by legendary artists such as Michelangelo and Raphael, but also by artists such as Mariotto Albertinelli and Fra Bartolomeo. Leonardo da Vinci powered through this period by creating many famous works such as *The Last Supper*, the *Mona Lisa*, and *Saint John the Baptist*. However, the High Renaissance was much more than artistic growth. There were major political and religious shakeups that shifted power and cultural focus among the people. Religious fervor and apocalyptic beliefs came to a head during this time and created a spiritual bottleneck. There were building blocks over several thousand years that led to this brilliant period that vanished all too quickly.

---

11. Jansen, *Making of the Magdalen: Preaching and Popular Devotion in the Later Middle Ages*, 151.

CHAPTER 16

The Trial

THE FIRST COUNCIL OF Nicaea materialized in 325 under Roman Emperor Constantine I. Despite occurring 80 years before Saint Jerome created the Vulgate, it was meant to debate the nature of Jesus Christ. Its primary concern was the growing controversy surrounding Arianism which challenged Christ's divinity. Arianism rejects the concept of the Holy Trinity and believes Jesus to be a creation of God, but not God himself. Therefore, they believe that only God is separate from existence, which makes Jesus a human creature.[1] They believe Jesus is independent from God because he only existed through God's demand. This theology caused the Arians to flirt with polytheism.[2] The First Council of Nicaea condemned Arianism as heretical, and many were exiled. While this is the catalyst for years of theological warfare, ultimately the goals of the Council won and became a permanent fixture of Christian doctrine.

Roman Emperor Constantine I saw this schism playing out between the Christians who advocated for Christ's divinity and those who did not. Understanding this was a fragile ecosystem, Constantine saw that this could threaten stability. Getting ahead of any turmoil, he formed the First Council of Nicaea in 325, which he attended. Constantine was not a Christian then and was not baptized until on his deathbed in 337. Constantine

---

1. Britannica Editors, "Arianism," lines 17–19.
2. Britannica Editors, "Arianism," lines 22–25.

formed the First Council of Nicaea for political security, not because of any personal beliefs he had regarding Christ. His baptism shortly before his death was meant to stabilize the Roman Empire, which his sons, Constantine II, Constantius II, and Constans, later ruled. As per Roman tradition, upon Constantine I's death, posthumous coins featuring his likeness were issued. They depicted Constantine I as a deity. His deathbed baptism was politically motivated as Constantine, and those closest to him still viewed him as a divine figure.

While the First Council of Nicaea was ultimately successful, Arianism and Gnosticism remained popular. The Gnostic Gospel, The Life of John the Baptist, was written in 390 through the voice of Saint Serapion of Thmuis. Saint Serapion is known for being an opponent of Arianism, so it is peculiar why a Gnostic Gospel is attributed to him. Christian scholar, Tony Burke, has deciphered much of this work. One of the plots is that after John the Baptist is beheaded, his head flies around the world for several years preaching God's Word and criticizing Herod. After this floating head completed its evangelizing it was buried in Homs (Emesa), while his body was buried in the town of Sebaste.[3] Centuries later, the Knights Templar, Knights Hospitaller of Saint John the Baptist, and other Crusaders passed through this town. So, while the First Council of Nicaea drew a clear line in the sand for Christian theology, new Gnostic Gospels were still coming out, and much older Gnostic Gospels remained prominent. It took Saint Jerome's Vulgate to solidify a traditional Christian theology.

Just as how the First Council of Nicaea was established to resolve theological mysteries, many questions today remain regarding the assassination of Daphne Galizia. Charges have been filed, and convictions have been made. However, other potential suspects are walking freely. Galizia made enemies and she had many lawsuits pending against her. This means that there could be several potential suspects. When she was alive she was regularly harassed, and prior threats of violence ultimately led the authorities nowhere. But how far would someone who had previously threatened her really go? Would they go to the lengths of orchestrating a car bomb? Or did their threats simply stop after posting on social media? The government of Malta knew she was a high-profile target with increasingly more enemies than friends. Yet they did not provide her with necessary protection, even

---

3. Burke, "More Christian Apocrypha Updates 13: Life of John the Baptist by Serapion," lines 1–24.

though she was probably more of a target than many Maltese politicians themselves. Nevertheless, some convictions have at least been made.

Vincent Muscat (no relation to former Prime Minister Joseph Muscat) pleaded guilty in 2021 to assisting with the car bomb that killed Galizia in 2017. He was only sentenced to 15 years in prison.[4] Relief for Galizia's family was only found when he pleaded guilty. However, anger still resided because of the light sentence he received compared to the crime he had confessed to. According to the police, they believe he operated as a contract killer, not as someone who had a personal vendetta against Daphne. A reason for his lenient sentencing is that he received a pardon in exchange for assisting authorities in a separate assassination case. This other unsolved case involves the 2015 murder of lawyer, Carmel Chircop.[5] As of 2025, the Chircop case has still not been solved. Vincent Muscat also seems to be having a tough time in prison. In 2023 he had an additional 7 months added to his 15-year sentence for getting in a fight and biting a fellow inmate.[6]

Several other arrests have been made regarding the Galizia case. Brothers Adrian and Robert Agius, and their partner Jamie Vella, have been held in jail since 2021.[7] These three men are accused of supplying the bomb used for the murder. However, even though they have been charged, they have not received a trial at the time of this writing. The people of Malta are left with increasing frustration as there has not been any movement on this case. Local reporting on these three has been minimal as transparency appears to be lacking in the Maltese courts. Having been arrested in 2021, they have been sitting in a jail cell for years. Speculation is only mounting for the three of them with each day that passes. Most importantly, the family of Daphne Galizia is being prevented from receiving any real closure by not having a trial.

Galizia wrote frequently about the corruption at the highest levels that plagued Malta. One of the last things she wrote was that *there are crooks everywhere you look now*. She was killed a few hours later. Almost 5 years after her assassination, another set of brothers, George and Alfred

4. Garside, "Man guilty of Daphne Caruana Galizia murder given 15-year sentence," lines 1–3.

5. Garside, "Man guilty of Daphne Caruana Galizia murder given 15-year sentence," lines 16–30.

6. Brincat, "Daphne hitman Vince Muscat gets seven-month sentence for biting prisoner," lines 1–3.

7. Garside, "Man guilty of Daphne Caruana Galizia murder given 15-year sentence," lines 7–10.

Degiorgio, were sentenced to 40 years in prison. Both pleaded guilty to the attack, however, matters regarding this have been complex. In the courtroom, George Degiorgio shouted at the prosecution while asking them if they knew who killed Daphne. Degiorgio's question was rhetorical as he then shouted that it was the courtroom's friends who killed her. With the government of Malta's lack of protection for Galizia, he wasn't entirely wrong. Speaking from a prison cell, George Degiorgio said that the murder of Galizia was *just business*.[8] Later, a disappointing, but not surprising, decision made by the Maltese courts, allowed George Degiorgio to leave prison to attend a family baptism celebration. It was reported that he had a great time and was all smiles while enjoying some drinks. Daphne's son, Matthew, described the moment as *Mafia Country*.[9]

An alleged mastermind behind the assassination is businessman Yorgen Fenech. In 2019, Prime Minister Joseph Muscat gave a presidential pardon to Melvin Theuma, an alleged middleman. In exchange for the pardon, Theuma supposedly provided the authorities with information regarding the case, including the engineer of the crime.[10] Yorgen Fenech was arrested shortly after this pardon. Once he was taken into custody, Fenech offered to be a witness and provide information. Nevertheless, Fenech remained in police custody. Yorgen Fenech vehemently denies being involved with Galizia's assassination. In 2024, former CEO of the Malta Gaming Authority (MGA), Heathcliff Farrugia, was found guilty of leaking documents to Fenech regarding an upcoming raid on a rival casino.[11] Corruption surrounds not only the people allegedly involved with the Galizia case, but Malta in general.

Over the years since his arrest, Yorgen Fenech has not received a trial. He made multiple attempts to be granted bail, but his requests have been denied. In 2024, Fenech's lawyers demanded he be released on bail since he had been jailed for over 30 months without a trial. Prosecutors stalled for years regarding this request and left it in the hands of the court system.[12]

8. Hilliar, "Brothers sentenced to 40 years in prison for murdering Maltese journalist Caruana Galizia," lines 1–35.

9. Balzan, "Jailed Daphne murderer allowed to attend family baptism party," lines 1–8.

10. Reuters, "Malta grants pardon to suspected middleman in journalist murder— police sources," lines 1–6.

11. Thomas-Akoo, "Ex-MGA CEO Farrugia found guilty of leaking secrets to Yorgen Fenech," lines 1–3.

12. Bil-Malti, "Yorgen Fenech says he should be granted bail because he has been in jail for 30 months," lines 1–10.

Fenech was ultimately granted bail in 2025. Even though there have been several convictions regarding Galizia's murder, none of the people found guilty have so far made public proclamations as to who engineered the attack. Public opinion is that Yorgen Fenech is the one who commissioned the car bomb, but this has yet to be tried in the court of law. Maltese citizens are losing hope as each day passes.

One of the judges involved with the Yorgen Fenech case is Chief Justice Mark Chetcuti. Recently he has recused himself from the case because he had been a part of the selection of a trial judge for it. A judge recusing himself is usually not controversial, and this is no different. However, the uneasy feeling Maltese citizens have over the Galizia case has grown into an understandable paranoia. On a separate trial, Chief Justice Mark Chetcuti rejected an appeal regarding the trafficking of ecstasy by Jean Marc Dalli in 2023. Dalli's mother is Helena Dalli, a European Union Commissioner and former Malta minister. Jean Dalli's father, Patrick Dalli, is an artist. When the decision by the court was read, Patrick Dalli caused a scene in the courtroom. During his tantrum he hurled accusations towards Chief Justice Mark Chetcuti of being in the mafia, the Freemasons, and Opus Dei.[13] Accusations such as this are common with the people of Malta. If they do not like someone, they will often make these proclamations. These declarations speak to the intermittent mass psychosis that stems from the corruption in the island nation. With justice for Daphne severely lagging, the entire country of Malta was about to crumble.

13. Agius, "Patrick Dalli insults Chief Justice in open court after son's drug trafficking statement deemed admissible," lines 36–48.

CHAPTER 17

Secretive Organizations

OPUS DEI IS A Catholic organization founded in 1928 by Father Josemaría Escrivá in Spain. They have been accused of various controversies, some of which are factual, and others having been fabricated. Public weariness of the organization has also grown in recent years because of fictionalized depictions of them. This is not a secret society. However, accusations of secretiveness have been levied against them for reasons that include not making their membership list public. The issue with allegations like this is that most organizations, religious or not, do not publicize active membership lists. Imagine if an organization such as the Elks Lodge was pressured into publicizing their membership list. It would be an absurd demand. Nevertheless, members of Opus Dei are free to make public about their involvement with the group and are never discouraged from doing so. That is all to say that controversies involving Opus Dei are ongoing.

The purpose of Opus Dei is to live a life devoted to God. Father Josemaría Escrivá, who entered sainthood in 2002, said that a love of Christ should expand beyond the boundaries of prayer. Father Escrivá proclaimed that God can be found through even our more mundane, daily tasks. There seems to be a movement with modern-day, non-denominational Christians emphasizing spiritual work through common duties. They say that God can be found by doing the laundry, exercising, or running errands for example. What most of these non-denominational Christians do not realize is that is the core concept created by Opus Dei. Some passages in the New Testament stress the need to find God in daily life. However, these concepts historically had never been put into practice until Opus Dei came into the picture. So, the popularization of this form of prayer made popular by non-denominational Christians is the work of the Catholic Opus Dei at its core.

I was fortunate to speak with a high-ranking member of Opus Dei, Father Bradley Arturi. One of the questions I asked him was if Opus Dei has a special focus on John the Baptist or any other saints. He informed me that they do not focus on sainthood any more or less than what Catholics already do. They pray to saints and celebrate them in accordance with the teachings of the Catholic Church. Another question I asked Father Arturi was about the charitable work they perform as an organization. Father Arturi first told me that he prefers to call volunteering and acts of charity as *Apostolic Works* instead. This is because the Opus Dei viewpoint is to practice prayer in every aspect of life. What intrigued me most was his later response that Opus Dei does not do these *Apostolic Works* in an organized sense. Instead, their members are encouraged to do this on their own or with other established organizations. In other words, you will not see an Opus Dei fundraiser to build a new park anytime soon.

Some members of Opus Dei choose to practice the mortification of the flesh. This practice has caused a great deal of scrutiny for obvious reasons. First, it must be called out that other religions use similar practices. A portion of Shiite Muslims today practice forms of bodily harm to mark their Holy Day of Ashura. During the Middle Ages, self-flagellation was also fairly common among Christians as an act of repentance. So, Opus Dei practicing forms of mortification is nothing new. It is also an act that is supported by the Vatican. Nevertheless, harming oneself to show how much they love their God is extreme. Members will cite that they are called to feel a portion of the pain that Christ felt on the Cross. However, other Catholics have argued that Jesus was tortured and killed so that we ourselves do not have to experience it.

Malta has a high percentage of Catholic citizens, so it makes sense that Opus Dei has a presence there. At the Church of Our Lady of Victory in 2008, Archbishop Monsignor Paul Cremona celebrated Mass in honor of Saint Escrivá. He stressed the importance of Opus Dei and for Catholics to take part in their message.[1] It should also be pointed out that the Church of Our Lady of Victory was built by the Knights Hospitaller of Saint John

---

1. Independent, "Everyone can be Holy," lines 1–30.

the Baptist in the 1500's. Regular services are held in honor of Saint Escrivá. Archbishop Charles Scicluna of Malta led the funeral for Daphne Caruana Galizia after her murder. He expressed great sadness over her death and proclaimed his support for the protection of journalists. Several years later in 2023, Archbishop Scicluna was accused, with zero evidence, of being a member of Opus Dei by a popular Maltese professor. In turn, accusations have been made against this professor claiming that he is in the mafia.[2] The cultural element in Malta of labeling enemies as being a member of Opus Dei, the Mafia, or Freemasonry is incredibly common. Most of the time these are false accusations.

Daphne Galizia had public arguments with Opus Dei such as a notable debate between Dr. Michael Asciak and herself. Dr. Asciak belongs to Opus Dei and is also a member of Parliament for the Nationalist Party Executive Committee in Malta. Galizia had written that members of Opus Dei should have no part in the Bioethics Committee and cited their religious fervor as her reasoning. Dr. Asciak responded by calling her *cynical* and that Catholic lay members can play as much, or as little, in society as everyone else.[3] This public quarrel gained much attention in Malta and opened a dialogue regarding bioethical stances on topics such as stem cell research and abortion. Daphne Galizia operated on occasion as an agitator. Her hurling Opus Dei accusations speak not only to this but also to the Maltese culture of using it as an insult. However, Opus Dei had nothing at all to do with her death. These publicly written debates never turned deadly.

I was able to speak with Dr. Asciak directly and he is proud to be a member of Opus Dei, despite the challenges it sometimes entails. Dr. Michael Asciak provided further clarification on Opus Dei and his involvement with the organization. Asciak said to me that it is true that members carry out their *Apostolic Work* through outside charities. However, they can also perform their own religious and social activities for members and friends, as well as anyone else who would like to attend. While charity is important to Opus Dei, friendship is the most central component. He went on to say that much of what is known about Opus Dei from the public is from fictionalized novels and television. I asked Dr. Asciak if he faced any scrutiny from Parliament over his membership, and he replied that he had not faced any direct criticism.

2. Balzan, "Curia shoots down blogger's 'false' claims on Alfred Sant's annulment," lines 44–49.

3. Asciak, "Daphne's Article is three years late," lines 1–46.

Freemasons have been scrutinized as well, especially since a high-profile individual claimed he was paid $100,000 by them to assist with the assassination of Galizia.[4] The Freemasons are a fraternal organization that has existed for centuries. Many famous, important men of history have been members such as President George Washington and the writer, Oscar Wilde. Throughout the world there are local factions that operate out of what is called a Lodge. Chances are you have seen these around where you live. Freemasons are typically not secretive about their locations either as they post their insignia for high visibility. Members simply apply for admission on their local chapter's website, then there is an initiation upon approval. From there, members pay dues and attend regular meetings. The unhinged belief that Freemasons *run the world* is absurd for plenty of reasons. One easy way to prove this is to become a member yourself to find out. It should be noted that this alleged payment of $100,000 was a false accusation. The Freemasons played no part in Galizia's assassination.

I do not mean to disparage all conspiratorial thinking. There have been a great number of actions that were deemed a conspiracy that turned out to be true. A couple of examples are *Operation Midnight Climax* and *Operation Paperclip*. What I take issue with is when a seemingly normal, average person makes an outlandish claim about something that they carry no inside knowledge of. Scrolling through social media and committing to a ton of Google searches is not insider knowledge. Whenever I come across a conspiratorial standpoint, I typically ask the question: *How do you know this information and I do not?* That question alone works for a wide variety of circumstances. If someone ever makes a claim that seems off to you, or if you suspect they are talking out of turn, simply ask them that question. They tend to freeze out of embarrassment.

Galizia had been critical of the Freemasons and wrote about them for decades. In 1991, she wrote a column titled *Spilling the masons' beans* for the Times of Malta. In this opinion piece, she challenged the alleged influence that the Freemasons carry. Another article from 2017 for her blog, *Running Commentary*, titled *So many Freemasons cluttered around Delia*, stated that at least one lawyer with a libel case pending against her was a Freemason. She was assassinated a month after this blog was posted. Daphne Galizia created many enemies with her writing. Often, she called out both individuals and groups for their alleged behavior. Galizia targeted

---

4. Magri, "Freemasons 'categorically' deny involvement in Daphne Caruana Galizia's murder," lines 13–14.

both Opus Dei and the Freemasons for what she viewed to be transgressions. There are thousands of Opus Dei and Freemason members around the world. Attempting to make connections when there is only circumstantial evidence at play is irresponsible. However, Daphne Galizia was right to have moments of minor paranoia as her fateful end proved as such. In a desperate search for answers, people in Malta were quick to point the finger at Opus Dei and the Freemasons.

Straightforwardly, Opus Dei and the Freemasons had nothing to do with the murder of Daphne Galizia. Those so far that have been convicted, as well as those with alleged ties to them, are not members of either organization. In fact, in 2016, Opus Dei member, Dr. Michael Asciak wrote an article praising the work of Galizia.[5] Since her death, Dr. Asciak has written additional articles about how her assassination was an atrocity, and that he stands in solidarity with her. As far as the Freemasons go, they provided helpful resources and immediately outright condemned the attack. The alleged payment of $100,000 by a Freemason for her assassination turned out to be a complete lie as well.[6] People regularly make conspiratorial accusations against the Freemasons. Galizia being specifically targeted by them does not pass any logical standards.

Historic contempt and unsettledness from Maltese citizens against Opus Dei and the Freemasons make sense on the surface. One group is a hardline Catholic organization with members in the government. The other is a pay-for-play fraternal order that has secret meetings at night. Anyone who lacks decent critical thinking faculties and has an internet connection can put together puzzle pieces that are not actually there. It is then further compounded when an acclaimed investigative journalist not only plays into these conspiracies but ends up being murdered as well. Evidence and motivation are lacking in Opus Dei and the Freemasons being involved with her murder. Muddied and cherry-picked evidence does not equate to the truth. While more questions than answers remain about Daphne Galizia, a junk theory is never an adequate one.

5. Asciak, "Good and bad people in government," lines 1–3.
6. Magri, "Freemasons 'categorically' deny involvement in Daphne Caruana Galizia's murder," lines 1–18.

CHAPTER 18

New World Order

COGNITIVE-ASSOCIATED REASONING DOES NOT always compute that the voyages of Christopher Columbus occurred during the High Renaissance. In 1492, the year Columbus set sail, Leonardo da Vinci was living in Milan, where he completed his famous *Vitruvian Man* drawing. So many remarkable things were happening during this time that it can be overwhelming to process it. Christopher Columbus was not the only explorer of this period either. While Columbus was the most impressive of this lot, he set sail during the Age of Discovery when there were many other explorers. News about these explorations traveled rapidly through the printing press and word-of-mouth. Everyone knew that finding land masses involved deadly risks. Leonardo da Vinci and his associates certainly knew about these voyages and what they had uncovered. Christopher Columbus sought to explore the world, while Leonardo da Vinci sought to explore the arts and sciences.

We do not know much about the early life of Christopher Columbus. It is believed that he was born in 1451 in the Republic of Genoa and that he had several brothers and sisters. According to his notebooks, Columbus first set sail at the age of 14 and found an immediate love for it. Setting sail in the modern age is dangerous enough, but back in the 1400's it was a venture for only the bravest. There was no technology, no stress signals, and no proper medicine. If something went wrong on that ship, you had to do your best and hope for the best. Today we have cruise ships and people that go sailing as a leisurely activity. But in the era of Columbus, setting sail had to be your calling. Being on a boat in the middle of the ocean, leaving everything you know behind, takes great courage. Much criticism comes from lazy people who wear sweatpants all day and scroll on their phones over the weekend. These indolent critics could never display a fraction of the bravery that Columbus exhibited on his voyages.

Between 1492 and 1504, Christopher Columbus led 4 separate expeditions to the New World. It is true that there have been other visits to this new land mass by other explorers. What sets Columbus apart is that he was the first explorer to establish a lasting presence. Previous explorers established a minimal presence, and there were little to no writings about their time spent there. This is why many nations from the United States to Colombia and several countries in the Caribbean all celebrate Columbus Day. Not to lean too much into a cliché, but Christopher Columbus was a man of his time. What was deemed appropriate and acceptable for someone in the 1400's is remarkably different for someone living in the 21st century. If we judge the great men of history only on the bad things they had done, we would be left with few to celebrate.

Broad negative narratives have been hurled against Christopher Columbus by modern political activists. Much of their claims either exaggerate or outright refuse to look at Columbus in the full context of history. An example is that Columbus did send slaves from the New World back to Spain. This is irrefutable. What also needs to be mentioned is that this was part of the deal. He would not have received the necessary support from the Spanish Crown if he did not agree. This was the political reality of that time, and it was a terrible thing. But it is a reality, nonetheless. To place this in a broader context, the tribes Columbus encountered also practiced slavery within their population. Furthermore, the Aztecs sacrificed between 10,000 and 80,000 people over 4 days at the re-consecration of the Great Pyramid of Tenochtitlan in 1487. Human sacrifice, torture, rape, and cannibalism were a part of daily life for the early inhabitants of the New World.[1] Again, we are only products of the time in which we are living. The 1400's was a particularly brutal period.

After arriving back in Spain from his first voyage, Columbus wrote a letter regarding his discoveries to the Spanish Crown. First written in Spanish, the letter was then sent to Rome where it was printed in Latin. From there it was printed in several other languages and dispersed throughout

---

1. Hassig, "sacrificio y las guerras floridas," 1–47.

Europe.[2] The sheer number of copies, as well as being printed in multiple languages, made the New World a well-known subject during this time. The news of Columbus spread rapidly. There were also more explorers than just Christopher Columbus. Portuguese explorer Bartolomeu Dias discovered the southern tip of Africa in 1488, and Vasco da Gama made the first direct voyage from Europe to India in 1498. There were plenty of other explorers during this time and they all contributed to this longing to discover the unknown parts of the world.

Although Leonardo da Vinci's thoughts on these discoveries are unknown, he certainly was aware of them. This period led to an age of not only excitement but also hesitancy for the unknown. The world that Leonardo grew up in was rapidly expanding. Regardless of how specific information he may or may not have known, hearing about these discoveries would have been earth-shattering. A hypothetical modern equivalent is if sea explorers discovered an entire civilization under the ocean. Many people of the High Renaissance were now reflecting on their own lives and their place in the world. For someone like da Vinci, these explorations would have posed deep questions about his existence. But regardless of what was going on at the time, for a faithfully baptized Catholic, the only thing that ultimately mattered was reaching Heaven.

Even though da Vinci knew about these discoveries, some researchers have sought to embellish more than we can prove. Stefaan Missinne is a professor and Fellow of the Royal Geographical Society in London. He also studied directly under Professor Carlo Pedretti, a late authority on da Vinci scholarship. Missinne took the New World discovery a step further by claiming Leonardo mapped the New World. Not only does he say that da Vinci drew the map, but that this map was originally misread as a depiction of the moon. I must say that looking at this drawing of da Vinci's it does look like it could be a map. Stefaan Missinne expands on this assumption by proclaiming da Vinci then sculpted a globe that depicts the North American continent. No known da Vinci sculpture still exists, and not one legitimate da Vinci scholar thinks that he made this globe. Nevertheless, Missinne was able to publish his findings in an academic journal.[3] The only problem with this theory is that none of it is true or backed by any evidence.

---

2. Lehrman, "Columbus reports on his first voyage, 1493," 12–20.

3. Missinne, "Leonardo Depicted America: Misread as the Moon," lines 1–9.

A person making a claim is the one responsible for providing the evidence. The burden of proof falls on them. It is not the other person's responsibility to disprove a claim that they hear. Evidence is all that matters in the end and Stefan Missinne does not provide any actual evidence. His foundation lies in his opinion of a small aspect of the *Salvator Mundi* painting. One problem with this is that most da Vinci scholars question if Leonardo even made the *Salvator Mundi*. Therefore, Missinne is merely giving an opinion on a painting that most likely was not painted by Leonardo. His entire theory of this map and globe depends on it. The theory becomes more absurd when he claims that the three dots in the crystal orb of the *Salvator Mundi* look like a constellation that explorers may have seen. This is not evidence as he is putting his own interpretation on the meaning behind three specks of paint.

Other problems presented in Missinne's research paper include but are not limited to, misspellings and formatting irregularities. He also cites himself four times in his research. Citing yourself even once is one time too many. Out of the books, academic research papers, and opinion columns I have written over the years, not once have I ever cited myself. Missinne did it four times in a single paper. A final call out is that towards the end of his paper, he declares that there is no conflict of interest in his research. I dug a little deeper and found that to be a false claim as well. It turns out that the owner of the globe he believes da Vinci sculpted is none other than Stefaan Missinne himself.[4] Missinne stands to gain tens, if not hundreds, of millions of dollars if he was in possession of a true da Vinci sculpture. Just because there is academic research that backs a claim does not always mean that the claim is true.

We know that da Vinci was aware of the discovery of new land masses, but we do not know his thoughts regarding these discoveries. However, even without knowing his specific feelings on the matter, it is without question that it impacted him. It impacted everyone at the time. People's understanding of the world had opened up to be even grander than ever before. Brave explorers like Christopher Columbus helped to create this new reality. People no longer felt trapped on their own land mass as sailing the seas and oceans now confirmed to lead to new land. The world no longer seemed to have an *end* to it, but rather only new beginnings. It should also be noted that when Christopher Columbus reached the island of what

---

4. Orland, " 'da Vinci Globe': A chance discovery," lines 1–21.

is now known as Puerto Rico, he named it San Juan Bautista, translated in English to mean Saint John the Baptist.

While setting sail serves various purposes, such as exploration of new land, it can also serve as a means of escape. According to the Italian Dominican friar, Jacobus de Voragine (1230-1298), in his written work *Golden Legend* (1265), Mary Magdalene is forced on a rudderless boat by pagans and set sail with the hopes of her perishing. However, she and the others on the boat survived and washed ashore in southern France. According to Voragine's *Golden Legend*, Mary Magdalene convinces the King of France not to kill them and ends up performing a variety of miracles. While the *Golden Legend* is not scripturally based, it was an incredibly popular story and provided context to religious scripture. These tales have also created even further legends regarding Mary Magdalene's royal bloodline with Jesus Christ. One of them is that Jesus and Mary Magdalene's daughter, Sarah, married into French royalty. This secret lineage later married into the Merovingian Dynasty. The holy bloodline supposedly lives on to this very day.

While a fanciful story, its source material carries a deep history. Not only does the inspiration for the *Golden Legend* come from other Dominican friars, but Voragine also pulls from a Gnostic text known at the time called the Gospel of Nicodemus. While this Gnostic Gospel was written as early as the 4th century, it is believed that its oral tradition goes much farther back. The *Golden Legend* was also pulled from the written histories by Gregory of Tours (538–594) for inspiration. In addition, the *Golden Legend* pulls references from John Cassian (360–435), an influential mystical Christian monk. So, while this story rests more in the field of myth and legend, it stems from much older written works whose own stories come from ancient oral traditions. This speculative history compounded with other archaic oral and written legends, creates powerful stories.

Stemming from the *Golden Legend*, additional ancient myths have developed around Mary Magdalene sailing away from persecution. One is the story of the Three Marys being on the fleeing boat that washed up along the shores of southern France. The identity of the Three Marys is debated, but it is commonly understood that Mary Magdalene was one of them. This story states that this rudderless boat contained the Three Marys as well as a little girl named Sarah. This girl makes her first known written appearance in Vincent Philippon's 1521 book, *The Legend of the Saintes-Maries*. While not an official saint in the Roman Catholic Church, Sarah is considered a saint among Folk Catholicism and the Romani people. She represents the oppressed and displaced, just as the legend of her arrival in France suggests. A large shrine of Saint Sarah is in the Church of the Saintes Maries de la Mer in the French coastal town of Saintes-Maries-de-la-Mer. The name of this town is translated to mean *The Saint Marys of the Sea*.

In ancient Hebrew, the name Sarah means princess. People have pondered just who this young girl on the boat with the holy women was. Was she a servant, or something else? With ancient stories, as well as the meaning of her name, some have suggested that she was the daughter of Mary Magdalene and Jesus Christ. When comparing the canonical Gospels and the Gnostic Gospels, combined with old stories such as the *Golden Legend*, it appears plausible. The prominent issue that arises from this is the assumption that the tales are true. If you take the context clues from the Gnostic Gospels and other written material, then sure, it could be factual. However, the Gnostic Gospels and various supplementary works are still controversial. So, while they do stem from rich oral traditions and written cross-references, they all have the same motivation in pushing one specific narrative.

But it is not only the Gnostic Gospels that position Mary Magdalene as a person of special importance to Jesus. We can read it right in the passages of the Bible. Ancient sources often listed names starting with the most important person first. An exception to this is if the list of names were meant to be chronological, such as lines of genealogy found throughout the Old Testament. When Mary Magdalene is mentioned within a list, she is almost always placed right at the beginning. Here are some of these biblical verses, Matthew 27:56, Matthew 27:61, Matthew 28:1, Mark 15:40, Mark 15:47, Mark 16:1, Luke 8:2–3, and Luke 24:10. Mary Magdalene is also the first person that Jesus reveals himself to after his resurrection. Not to his disciples, not to his mother, but to Mary Magdalene. Clues such as this are why legends of them being married and having children have flourished. From there we find further stories of Mary Magdalene and her daughter escaping by setting sail across dangerous seas.

Brave explorers of the past set sail to discover new lands. It required a massive amount of courage as being stuck on a ship sailing towards the unknown promised little to no safety. From these explorations came many tall tales such as sea monsters and mermaids. But just because these stories come from ancient traditions, does not mean they are factual. This is similar to the story of the Three Marys and Saint Sarah arriving in France. Leonardo da Vinci was well aware of the discovery of new land masses by explorers, but the legends that had arisen from them do not seem to have impacted his work or himself as a person. The discovery of new land masses by explorers and the legend of the Three Marys and Saint Sarah arriving in fresh territory symbolizes not only new ground but new beginnings. John the Baptist represents similar concepts, however, his is one of a spiritual arrival. Leonardo da Vinci's painting of this prophet aims to depict this journey.

CHAPTER 19

Later Years

KING ARTHUR IS AN adventurous story concocted in the Middle Ages and became widely popular. Its stories of battles, romance, quests, and the powerful Knights of the Round Table, penetrated the hearts and minds of people across the land. They also believed these stories to be factual and were convinced of their authenticity well into the 18th century. Some of the reasons why they thought it to be true is because it stems from a rich oral tradition. From there it was written by several unrelated individuals, and their written work cross-checked each other's fairly well, even if there were some minor differences here and there. But the legend of King Arthur is entirely fictionalized as there isn't a single shred of evidence to prove any of these stories truly happened. Some credible historians suggest that there may have been some type of a King Arthur figure. However, the storylines around him are made up to tell a more entertaining story.

Mainstream Christianity rejects the so-called Gnostic Gospels under a similar premise of historians dismissing the historicity of King Arthur. Christians state that while the Gnostic Gospels stem from a deep oral tradition, and that they cross-check one another, there is no real historical basis for them to have occurred. Of course, this is the right assessment. But the issue that lies with them on this claim is that this same argument can be used against their beliefs as well. The Gospels of Matthew, Mark, Luke, and John also stem from an oral tradition, and their written texts do cross-reference themselves. The only dividing factor is that the early

Church leaders selected Matthew, Mark, Luke, and John, and rejected the other gospels. Theoretically if they added a fifth gospel, like the Gnostic Gospel of Mary, Christians would have to accept it. The reason for this is because Christians ultimately accept the books in the traditional Bible because that is what the early Church leaders had selected. There is no deeper reason other than that.

Christians who may push back on why certain gospels were selected and others were not selected should look at their accepted gospels. Matthew, Mark, and Luke are Synoptic Gospels because they are so similar. However, John is left out of this categorization because that gospel is quite different from the other three. Matthew and Luke are thought to have derived their material from a theoretical Q Source, as well as the Gospel of Mark. So, while there are still major contradictions within those three books, the general story is the same. The Bible is anything but perfect as it is a compilation of stories with the expressed goal of portraying Jesus as the Messiah. As with any other religious text, the stories must be over-the-top in their portrayals of holy figures.

The Gospel of John is a story all on its own compared to Matthew, Mark, and Luke. Just some of the stories mentioned in John that are nowhere to be found in the other three include, but are not limited to, Jesus turning water into wine and washing the feet of his disciples. Not only are the stories in the Gospel of John quite different from the other three, but the overall tone, structure, and focus are different. Biblical scholar, Keith Long has described the Gospel of John as if someone inserted a random leaflet in the Bible.[1] Despite the Gospel of John being different from the other three gospels, Christians still accept it just as much as the synoptic gospels. Christians welcome the Gospel of John simply because the early Church leaders accepted it, despite major differences.

Christians may claim they do not believe in the Gnostic Gospels because while the stories are almost parallel to Matthew, Mark, Luke, and John, they are not similar enough. However, they say this whole-heartedly while still accepting the Gospel of John. Religion is complicated, especially since people tend to believe ancient texts as an unadulterated truth. This is also why the story of King Arthur was viewed as an absolute truth for centuries. History is complex, and the history of Christianity is not immune. Some Gnostic Gospels have different focuses and incorporate different miracles, just as the Gospel of John does the same thing. Nevertheless, the

1. Long, "Synoptic Gospels & the Gospel of John: 7 Key Differences," lines 9–17.

Gnostic Gospels have the same characters, such as Mother Mary and the disciples. People tend to focus only on the differences between the Gnostic Gospels and the traditionally accepted ones but rarely talk about the similarities. There is no more or less historical truth between the traditional Gospels and the Gnostic Gospels, just as there is no more or less truth in the legend of King Arthur.

The legend of King Arthur and the Knights of the Round Table is an ancient story made popular in Geoffrey of Monmouth's Historia Regum Britanniae (History of the Kings of Britain). Written in 1136, it not only helped to popularize the myth of King Arthur but also contains the oldest known version of King Lear, which William Shakespeare later brought to fame. Later in the 12th century, the French writer Chrétien de Troyes added additional concepts to the story of King Arthur, including that of the Holy Grail. Arthurian legend states that the Holy Grail is a form of chalice with magical healing powers and is associated with the Last Supper of Jesus Christ. We do not know if the story of King Arthur left an impact on Leonardo da Vinci. What we do know is that the legend of King Arthur was written hundreds of years before the birth of da Vinci and was a popular story during the Florentine Renaissance. Despite not knowing his understanding of Arthurian myth, the parallels between this fictionalized story of the Holy Grail and Leonardo's search for beauty and perfection carry symbolic similarities.

Pairing the Gnostic Gospels with Arthurian legends of a Holy Grail is one of the reasons some believe the Knights Templar possessed a secret truth. Books such as *The Holy Blood and the Holy Grail*, *The Woman with the Alabaster Jar*, and *The Dreamer of the Vine* have penetrated our imaginations successfully. These books directly inspired Dan Brown's novel *The Da Vinci Code*, which further popularized concepts of a Jesus bloodline and the Holy Grail. While *The Da Vinci Code* is fictionalized, and the other books mentioned do not hold up well to academic scrutiny, they play a vital role in myths and legends. And while many historical positions in these books miss the mark, they bring up interesting questions such as Jesus possibly being married and fathering children. The search for deeper truths penetrates the human mind and can set forth a great adventure in its pursuit. The Merriam-Webster Dictionary's definition of a Holy Grail is *an object or goal that is sought after for its great significance.*[2] In many ways, my journey in decoding da Vinci's painting, *Saint John the Baptist*, is my Holy Grail.

2. Merriam-Webster Dictionary, "Holy Grail," line 1.

Da Vinci witnessed much over his life. He rose from being born an illegitimate child to spending time with royalty. Acquiring great wealth and influence, Leonardo was free to pick and choose what he wanted to partake in. Everyone who could afford his expertise wanted a piece of him. Leonardo learned much over the years and did not let the barriers of the period he lived in slow his imagination. For da Vinci, life was about turning imaginative thought into reality as his love for thinking and curiosity contributed to his success. Understanding the history of the Plague in Milan energized da Vinci more than ever. This was then compounded by living in an Age of Discovery. Regardless of the specific information Leonardo knew about these voyages, it was the biggest news of his day. Escaping death from the plague while living in a time of major land discoveries seems to have created more ambition for Leonardo than ever before.

Towards the end of his life, Leonardo da Vinci suffered a series of ailments that physically slowed him down. His mind, however, remained sharp and he continued to work on many projects. One of his fascinations was the ancient Greek challenge of attempting to square the circle. This is, of course, impossible because a square is not a circle for several reasons, one being that it cannot have the same measurements as a circle. He persisted in attempting to solve this problem up until his dying day. For da Vinci, it was much more about the attempts at discovery than it was about finding the answer. Leonardo had also been fascinated by the movement of water throughout his life. As a child, he played in shallow streams and tossed pebbles in them to watch how the water swirled. Throughout his notebooks, we see that he utilized his love of drawing whirling water in his paintings. In his *Saint John the Baptist* painting, the curls of the subject's hair directly correlate to the ripples of water he once played with.

Water is a theme of da Vinci's life that we see in other works of his as well. One example is that he created many water-related inventions such as diving suits and snorkels. Another aspect of Leonardo's life that is not regularly discussed is that he had a penchant for writing fables. Being an admirer of the ancient Greek writer, Aesop, da Vinci followed suit and many of his short stories involved water. One of his fables, *The Donkey and the Ice*, tells the tragic story of ice that turns to water while a donkey stands on it. There has been minimal effort by scholars to translate his fables from Old Italian to any other language, including English. However, Bruno Nardini translated these written works and published them in the 1973 book, *Fables of Leonardo da Vinci*. Nardini took liberties with these translations by extending their length and embellishing the storyline. For example, da Vinci's fable, *The Donkey and the Ice*, in its original format is two sentences long with no quotations. The Nardini translation is about thirteen sentences with two separate quotations.[3]

Enhanced translations take the original voice out of the work. Leonardo da Vinci's fables were concise and carried a unique sting to them. Bruno Nardini seems to have attempted to decorate these fables for a modern audience with the hopes of creating a broader appeal. Caution should be self-issued when reading translations because of the liberties a translator may take. Nevertheless, the heart of the messaging in da Vinci's fables is still prevalent. Other fables of his that deal with water are *The Stream* and *The Water*. This running theme found in his inventions, art, and fables correlate to baptism. Just as John the Baptist washed away sins with water, this same element makes repeated appearances throughout Leonardo's work. Da Vinci never published his fables, nor was he commissioned for them. Instead, they are written as almost personal reminders to himself as a form of guidance.

Leonardo da Vinci became friends with Charles II d'Amboise who commissioned him for several projects. Charles II d'Amboise was a French nobleman and Governor of Milan. Da Vinci always had a proximity to power. One of these projects commissioned by d'Amboise was for Leonardo to be the architect of a palace for d'Amboise.[4] This is further evidence that even though da Vinci was getting older, he was still highly sought after for complex projects. Like most of his inventions, this project never came to fruition. However, his genius was still much ahead of his time. His architectural designs, for example, display an elegant brilliance that would have been difficult for others of the period to process.[5] Charles II d'Amboise's uncle, Emery d'Amboise, was the 41st Grand Master of the Knights Hospitaller of Saint John the Baptist.[6] The influence of this saint saturated every aspect of da Vinci's life.

One commission that d'Amboise did not request from da Vinci was a portrait. Instead, he commissioned Bernardino de' Conti, a more traditional painter, for the artwork. There does not seem to be any animosity for

3. Nardini, *Fables of Leonardo da Vinci*, 36.

4. Heydenreich, "Second Florentine period (1500–08) of Leonardo da Vinci," lines 67–73.

5. Craven, "Leonardo's Last Years," lines 55–56.

6. Geneanet, "Charles II d'Amboise," line 1.

not getting this commission. But it does show that even in da Vinci's older age, he was still creating work that was ahead of his time. It is easy to look at art from the High Renaissance as traditional painting. But back then that was not the way that some of the art, including art by da Vinci, was viewed. Charles II was also an avid coin collector, hence why his portrait by Bernardino de' Conti features his side profile, just like a coin does.[7] Leonardo da Vinci lived in a tumultuous time, and because of this many of the high-ranking people he was patronized by were involved in the chaos. Charles II d'Amboise had ongoing power struggles against the Catholic Church and led forces against Pope Julius II. There is no known documentation regarding where da Vinci stood with this conflict.

In what is known as da Vinci's Second Milanese Period (1508–1513) he witnessed a siege in Milan. This was the city where da Vinci believed he would spend the rest of his life. Leonardo comfortably looked towards more innovative artistic techniques such as constructing a giant horse sculpture with intricate detailing. Projects such as this ceased when Milan was attacked. At the time, Milan was run by France, however, in 1512, the papal forces, Swiss, Spaniards, and the Venetians drove them out of power. Leonardo was now left without financial supporters.[8] At his age, Milan was supposed to be the place he settled permanently in. But now his future was in flux. Less than one year after the attack in Milan, Leonardo began his painting *Saint John the Baptist*. This painting stems from a period of great social turmoil. At a time in his life when things were supposed to be tranquil and easy for him, the established order had been disrupted. It was at that moment that da Vinci did what he does best, and that was to paint.

Lorenzo de' Medici's son, Giovanni, took the papacy and became known as Pope Leo X. Because of Leonardo's close ties to Lorenzo and the Medici family, an invitation was sent to da Vinci to join them in Rome at the Vatican. He stayed there from 1513 to 1516, and it was during those years that Leonardo painted *Saint John the Baptist*. Coming fresh off the war in Milan that blew his retirement plans apart, he made one of his best paintings. While da Vinci worked on this painting in Rome, he lived in the Belvedere Courtyard at the Apostolic Palace. This is the same location as the Vatican Secret Archives where I started this journey of decoding the *Saint John the Baptist* painting. The beginning of my research into this work of art was physically where Leonardo began the creation of that very painting.

7. Macapia, "Charles d'Amboise," lines 1–13.
8. Wallace, *World of Leonardo: 1452–1519*, 149.

Leonardo da Vinci eventually left Rome and moved to France at the request of the King of France, Francis I. Da Vinci spent his remaining years serving the King at his leisure for various projects including painting and architecture. Leonardo brought his *Saint John the Baptist* painting along with him. He is thought by many to have completed the painting in 1516. Around this time, he made a series of apocalyptic drawings. These sketches feature torrential downpours and fortresses being destroyed in the chaos. Christian obsession with the end times is nothing new and has been with these religious folk since the inception of their faith. According to the Pew Research Center, almost half of all American Christians believed they were living in the end times in 2022.[9] This belief was even more prominent during the Renaissance. Da Vinci had lived through some of the harshest moments in world history, and he is now facing death himself from old age. His painting *Saint John the Baptist* features the saint who promises an eternal reward through baptism. Now with these apocalyptic drawings, he seems to be waiting for this to be fulfilled.

Frank Zöllner is one of the leading da Vinci scholars in the world. I have had the pleasure of discussing art and Leonardo with him on several occasions. I spoke with him about this connection between *Saint John the Baptist* and these apocalyptic drawings. Zöllner said that he did not believe there to be a connection. However, he referred me to the work of another scholar, Frank Fehrenbach, who has done extensive research on these drawings. Fehrenbach is quite insightful regarding this research and what is immediately noticeable is his description of these apocalyptic drawings. He states that the angels are the only figures that seem to escape this deluge. Furthermore, he points out that the non-believers face the direst of consequences in these sketches. Da Vinci further sends a shower of fire onto the damned.[10] This then helps to prove that Leonardo's *Saint John the Baptist* painting reflects his thoughts on the apocalypse and how to be saved from it.

Being alive during the High Renaissance, it is likely that Leonardo believed the end of the world was upon him. All of the evidence that we have points to him being a Catholic, even though in his later years, he also fashioned himself as a philosopher. However, this never competed with his Catholic faith. When da Vinci was painting the *Saint John the Baptist,* he

---

9. Diamant, "About four-in-ten U.S. adults believe humanity is 'living in the end times,'" lines 6–23.

10. Fehrenbach, *Taking Flight: Leonardo's Childhood Memories,* 286–287.

knew that he only had a few years left in him. So, while he probably believed the end times were upon the world, he was also projecting his demise onto his apocalyptic drawings. Regardless of what he thought about this, it is clear that death was on his mind. Leonardo painted the one saint who provided the method for salvation, while also creating drawings of what happens to those who refuse this offer. Even though Leonardo continued to work tirelessly, he was also preparing for the end of his life in the only way he knew how: through his art.

CHAPTER 20

Leonardo's Influence

MICHEL DE NOSTREDAME, BETTER known as Nostradamus, was a Renaissance-aged astrologer and oracle. While there is no evidence that da Vinci and Nostradamus knew of one another, they were alive at the same time for several years. Nostradamus lived from 1503 to 1566, and his most famous work, *The Prophecies*, was not completed until 1555. This written work contains a series of vague prophecies of future events, many of which were apocalyptic. So just as da Vinci drew pictures of a Christian Apocalypse towards the end of his life, Nostradamus cryptically wrote about the apocalypse-adjacent in his book. Adding to this, John the Baptist believed that the end times were to happen when he was still alive. Towards the end of da Vinci's life, it looks as if he felt the same. The prophecies of Nostradamus also seem to allude to his thinking that great destruction would happen when he was alive. His perplexing prophecies are clearly not real prophecies. One of the ways in which we know this is because of how vague they are. They are so vague that they can be applied to practically anything that the reader wishes to apply them to.

But just because his magical prophecies are not real, does not mean that they should be dismissed entirely. This is because he was a prominent figure and his book, *The Prophecies*, had a major impact at the time. Plus, it is also entertaining to read. These writings of Nostradamus can also be taken symbolically, similarly to how the Apocalyptic drawings by da Vinci can be taken. Both of these men truly believed in their respective work. But for us, it is a great way to understand their mindset. Nostradamus' prophecies tell us that he believed his power to be on the level of gods. Regarding da Vinci's apocalyptic drawings, it shows us he was thinking about salvation which he believed could only be achieved through belief in Christ and the Sacrament of Baptism. Nostradamus is telling us his vision, while da Vinci is foreshadowing his.

Leonardo da Vinci's painting, *Saint John the Baptist*, was not an artwork that simply held a steady presence over the centuries. Rather it has created a major impact on the arts. John the Baptist is an important prophet in the Catholic faith and his saturated influence became a major reason why da Vinci painted the figure. Art historians have done an incredible job deciphering his *Mona Lisa* and *Lady with an Ermine*. But unfortunately, the analysis of *Saint John the Baptist* has been mild in comparison. We know that the person in the painting is representing John the Baptist. There are two major giveaways with this, the first one being that he is holding a reed cross. The second one is that he is draped in what appears to be animal skin or fur. These are standard depictions of him in traditional Renaissance works. However, if those two props are removed, this person could be both anyone and no one at the same time.

John's right index finger is pointing towards the sky, as seen in other depictions of the prophet before this one. It symbolizes to the viewer what is most important in this life, which is serving the Lord and spending eternity with him in Heaven. The finger pointing toward the heavens keeps the focus on God and reminds us that he is watching from above. In the Christian tradition, baptism and declared faith are central components for salvation. John the Baptist is the first member in the gospels to bring about this necessary act for securing this. There is also a calming presence in the painting. John is standing confidently, but the playful smile radiating off him creates a sense of calm for the viewer. He looks as though he is part human and part spirit. Instead of being a figure of nightmares, he is a welcomed dream for the faithful.

Before Leonardo's version, John the Baptist had been painted in one of two ways. The first way as a frail, stoic figure, and the second way as a crazed madman surviving off locusts and honey. Da Vinci painted him as a well-fed man with beautiful hair. Not to mention that most of his bare body is exposed, which is also scandalous in its very nature. This painting is estimated to have been worked on from 1513–1516. In 1515, Leonardo was further inspired when he sketched a drawing based on the painting. This sexually charged drawing is titled *Angelo Incarnato* and is nearly identical to his *Saint John the Baptist* painting. The only catch is that he is not holding a cross, and no fur is covering his genitals. Instead, John is entirely nude in this painting and has an exposed erection. This is also one of the many pieces of evidence of Leonardo da Vinci's homosexuality.

Bernardino Luini was a student of Leonardo da Vinci and created remarkable works of art. You can easily see the influence da Vinci had on his paintings, particularly with his 1510 work, *Madonna del Roseto*. This is a prime example of the use of sfumato and creates an almost three-dimensional aspect of the figures. Luini's painting, *Angel of Annunciation* is a work that is directly inspired by da Vinci's painting, *Saint John the Baptist*. In addition to this, however, it is almost nearly identical to da Vinci's *Angelo Incarnato* drawing. The hair, the facial features, and the overall pose directly match. What appears to be the only change is that Luini's painting has John the Baptist covered in a robe. Da Vinci's artwork was inspired by his personal life and the world around him. From there, other artists drew direct inspiration from him.

Da Vinci's sexual preferences are more than just an interesting tidbit about his personal life. Regarding the *Saint John the Baptist* painting, however, it is a major clue as to why he depicted him in such a fashion. Other evidence that we have of Leonardo's homosexuality is that he never married or had any children. Even men who preferred other men still tended to get married and have children. Leonardo did not follow suit. There is also a drawing in his notebooks of a penis with legs walking towards a male buttock that is labeled as *Salai*. Furthermore, many other homoerotically charged drawings and paintings came from da Vinci and his workshop. A subtle drawing from 1495 titled *Heads of an Old Man and a Youth* further expounds on this. This depicts two men, one older and the other younger, standing close together and facing one another. The lower half of their chests and stomachs are not only pressed together but seem to be interconnected. Throughout his notebooks, it is also clear that Leonardo preferred to draw men in the nude much more than he did of women.[1]

No serious da Vinci scholar thinks he was straight. It is commonly understood that he had a sexual preference for men and that this influenced his depiction of John the Baptist. However, if one is still not convinced by this evidence, there is additional proof to support the claim. When da Vinci was 23 years old, he, along with three other men, was accused of sodomy.

---

1. Fiore, "6 Things You Don't Know about Leonardo da Vinci," lines 188–198.

However, this charge wasn't just between the four of them but also included a male prostitute named Jacopo Saltarelli. The only reason why da Vinci and the other men were never prosecuted is because one of them had connections to the powerful Medici family. A few weeks later a second accusation of sodomy was hurled against the four of them. However, the accuser never came forward and the case was ultimately dropped again.[2]

Saint John the Baptist welded together da Vinci's sexuality with his devoted Catholic faith. These two characteristics are not compatible with one another. However, da Vinci was a complicated and complex man which is why we are left with *Saint John the Baptist* being such an intricate work. The profound nature of this painting inspired many more of his contemporaries as well. Salai made a painting of John the Baptist with direct inspiration from the da Vinci version. Giampietrino, a follower of da Vinci's work, also created an inspired version of the painting. Centuries later, modern artists are still intrigued by Leonardo's painting. In 1988, Jeff Koons created a porcelain sculpture directly based on the painting by Leonardo da Vinci. *Saint John the Baptist* impacted artists the moment it was made and continues to do so to this very day. The painting is of Nostradamus-like proportions.

---

2. Fiore, "6 Things You Don't Know about Leonardo da Vinci," lines 167–175.

CHAPTER 21

Daphne's Legacy

DANTE ALIGHIERI'S WRITTEN WORK, the *Divine Comedy*, is a bridge between the Knights Templar and Leonardo da Vinci regarding the influence of Saint John the Baptist. In Dante's epic poem, a character mentioned throughout goes by the name Beatrice. It is thought that Beatrice was a real woman of history who Dante loved from afar. Scholarly debate is still ongoing with whether or not the literary Beatrice was in fact modeled after his real lost love. Regardless, Dante put the character Beatrice on a high-pedestal and portrayed her as almost on the same level of Jesus Christ. In the *Divine Comedy*, Beatrice is more than just a character, she is an idealized goddess. She is divine grace. A prophet. A savior. We do not know why Dante wrote about her in such an idealized way, but we certainly catch ourselves occasionally placing people we may know in a different class than what they may not deserve. Daphne Galizia's journalistic endeavors were noble and courageous. But not every story was right. She wasn't perfect. In many ways, Galizia is our modern-day Beatrice for journalism. Galizia left a profound impact on the world, but a human impact, not a godly one.

Malta has a deep history of assassinations. Bontadino de Bontadini was a member of the Knights Hospitaller of Saint John the Baptist. He had a brilliant mind and had various pursuits from engineering and architecture to the arts. Most well-known for creating the *Wignacourt Aqueduct*, he is a popular historical figure for Malta. However, in 1620 Bontadini was assassinated by Ferrante Marangio. The assassin was hired by the Knights

Hospitaller of Saint John the Baptist to carry out the attack. However, the reason for the murder is unknown.[1] Another member of the Knights Hospitaller, Sylvain de Bosredon, was killed in 1798 by Maltese rebels. Bosredon, who was also an artist, was accused of collaborating with the French during their occupation of Malta. The prominence of the Knights Hospitaller in Malta has remained strong over the centuries, even despite assassinations such as these.

Other prominent assassinations in Malta include the murder of 15-year-old Karin Grech. In 1977, Grech opened a package delivered to her home in Malta which turned out to be a letter bomb. To this day the case remains unsolved. However, the police and journalists believe it to be connected to a major doctor's strike that was occurring at the time. Grech's father was a physician who did not take part in the strike and was viewed by some as being a traitor to the movement. On the same day, another letter bomb was mailed to another doctor, however, that bomb did not detonate.[2] At the funeral of Karin Grech, Archbishop Mikiel Gonzi proclaimed that the attack on her was the first terrorist act in Malta. Archbishop Mikiel Gonzi was a member of the Knights of Malta, formerly known as the Knights Hospitaller of Saint John the Baptist. He was high up in their ranks as well, holding the position of Bailiff Grand Cross. Gonzi passed away in 1984 at the age of 98.

Raymond Caruana was a political activist and supporter of Malta's Nationalist Party (NP). He was murdered in a drive-by shooting in 1986. While closure has never been fully brought to this case, the car utilized was owned by the Malta Labour Party. Another high-profile assassination took place in 1995 when Islamic terrorist, Fathi Shaqaqi, was neutralized by two Mossad agents outside of a hotel in Sliema, Malta. Assassinations have a steady presence in this tiny island nation. Every murder, every accusation of corruption, and every crime that happens there rings loudly because of their small population. But murder and overall crime, is incredibly low in Malta. According to the University of Malta, every year from 1970–2018 there had been less than 5 murders per year.[3] Therefore, every assassination in Malta is greatly magnified.

1. Bonello, *Bontadino de Bontadini—The Murder of the First Baroque Architect in Malta*, 44–61.

2. Calleja, "The bomber who killed Karin Grech 'was a loner,'" lines 1–68.

3. Calafato, "Homicide Trends in Malta from 1970–2018: First Findings," lines 1–160.

Daphne Galizia was not killed in a unique way. Targeted bombing is an unfortunate reality in Malta. From 2010 through 2017 alone there were nineteen bombs set off targeting individuals. Many of these attacks are still unsolved.[4] It is challenging to contextualize Malta as having a low murder rate while simultaneously dealing with high-profile assassinations and targeted bombings. Malta is unique in this regard. It is also why the attack on Daphne Galizia is so prominent. Not only was it a transgression against free speech, but it was heinously carried out in a quiet, peaceful village. This is one of many reasons why Galizia's legacy loudly lives on and carries such a profound influence around the world.

In the years since her murder, journalists still come together to show their solidarity for Galizia. To this day they make public declarations about her bravery and the necessity of her work. Furthermore, they seek to find the people responsible for her murder and have them publicly prosecuted. Since the attack on Galizia, journalists have had a hyperfocus on Malta's lack of protection for investigative journalists. Their concerns were vindicated when in September 2024, Malta imposed a ban on all publications regarding Daphne Galizia outside of related court hearings.[5] A country that has freedom of speech, does not have it in the same way as the United States. It is rulings such as this that can take an investigative journalist to become a necessary agitator. This explains Daphne Galizia's approach to journalism. For her work to become widespread, she knew that she had to be direct with her reporting.

Several positive things have at least come out following her death. Posthumously, Galizia has been given dozens of honors and awards. A couple of these awards were receiving *Person of the Year* by La Repubblica in Italy, as well as the Conscience-in-Media Award by the American Society of Journalists and Authors. The Daphne Caruana Galizia Foundation was also created which aims to not only protect investigative journalists but also go after perpetrators that attack them. This organization is run in part by Galizia's husband and adult children. There is also the Daphne Caruana Galizia Prize for Journalism which awards prize money to journalists in the European Union for their reporting. Nothing can bring Galizia back, and no awards can make up for this horrendous crime. However, we can see

4. Pace, "Malta's Explosive History: 19 Bomb Attacks Since 2010," lines 1–5.

5. Vincent, "Malta: Seven years on, the murder of Daphne Caruana Galizia highlights continued need for reform," lines 1–30.

through these awards and her foundations the positive impact that Galizia left on the world.

Daphne Caruana Galizia left an indelible mark on promoting freedom of speech and fighting corruption. She was both relentless and fearless in her reporting. Uncovering high-level corruption, organized crime, and money laundering in Malta earned her fame and notoriety. Galizia's blog *Running Commentary* sheds light on scandalous stories such as the Panama Papers. I recommend visiting this blog to read her stories for yourself. Galizia's assassination in 2017 was an absolute tragedy. It righteously sparked worldwide outrage and calls for justice. This ultimately cemented Daphne Galizia as a champion of truth and accountability. It is also why she has been placed on a level of journalistic devotion, similar to what Dante did with Beatrice. Despite this, her influence extends far beyond Malta and has inspired many investigative journalists around the globe to continue their essential work.

CHAPTER 22

Modern Day Knighthood

IN MALTA'S CAPITAL, VALLETTA, is Saint John's Co-Cathedral. This enormous church was built between 1573 and 1578 by the Knights Hospitaller of Saint John the Baptist. Their leader at the time, Grand Master Jean de la Cassière, commissioned the famous Maltese architect Girolamo Cassar for the project. Grand Master Jean de la Cassière is buried in its crypt. The exterior of the church is in a Mannerist style, while the interior became Baroque following renovations in the 17th century. The interior of Saint John's Co-Cathedral is widely considered to be one of the greatest examples of Baroque architecture in all of Europe.[1] Judging from the name it should go without saying that the Knights Hospitaller dedicated this church to Saint John the Baptist. Saint John's Co-Cathedral is a testament to the rich history of the Knights of Malta.

For the first 100 years of the church's existence, its interior was decorated rather modestly. A likely reason for this is because it was quickly built following the Great Siege of Malta. In an act of defiance, this cathedral helped to symbolize their strength, and decorations were not a priority for the Knights. But in the 1660's, Grand Master Raphael Cotoner desired the church to be decorated in such a way that it competed with the Vatican. He put the talented artist, Mattia Preti, in charge of this design and it was he who gave it the Baroque style that the church is so widely known for.

---

1. Degiorgio, *Palaces and Lodgings of the Knights of St John at Malta*, 220–228.

The Knights Hospitaller used this cathedral as their main church for over 200 years until they were briefly expelled during the French occupation in 1798. Its interior later suffered minor damage during the bombing campaigns of World War II.[2] This church also houses a painting by one of the most famous artists of all time.

Caravaggio's painting, *The Beheading of Saint John the Baptist* (1608), resides in the cathedral. The Knights Hospitaller of Saint John the Baptist commissioned Caravaggio for the work, and it became the largest altarpiece he ever created.[3] This painting has a dark, almost black background in which the figures seem to be encased. The method for this technique is called chiaroscuro and was popularized by Leonardo da Vinci. This method is central to the creation of da Vinci's *Saint John the Baptist* painting. Caravaggio later incorporated chiaroscuro to become his signature style. It is the only painting of his that he ever signed. This church also houses another painting by Caravaggio titled *Saint Jerome Writing* (1607–1608). Caravaggio briefly served as a member of the Knights Hospitaller of Saint John the Baptist. However, the same year upon completing his altarpiece for the cathedral he got into a fight with, and seriously wounded, another Knight. He was then imprisoned for his actions but escaped shortly after. Caravaggio died in 1610 under unknown circumstances in Tuscany.

The Knights Hospitaller of Saint John the Baptist still exists to this very day. Their direct line, from its inception around 1099 to the present day, has never been broken. However, over the years there have been various orders that claim a right to the line of succession. Most of these claims have been outright rejected and not recognized. However, the Protestant Alliance of the Orders of Saint John of Jerusalem is a version that is recognized. Originally known as the Knights Hospitaller of Saint John the Baptist, they are now collectively known as the Knights of Malta. Membership includes individuals from royal families. Today this chivalric order focuses primarily on charitable efforts and does not operate militarily, although they do have strong connections to militaries from many nations. As of 2025 they have over 13,000 members and operate in many countries around the globe. They are arguably the most influential chivalric order in existence.

Chivalric Orders are loosely based on military orders with a Catholic foundation. Legitimate Orders tend to have been founded during the

2. Sammut, "Restoration work on central part of façade of St John's Co-Cathedral in Valletta complete," lines 45–46.

3. Pomella, *Caravaggio: An Artist through Images*, 106.

Crusades, such as the Knights Templar, with chivalric standards at the forefront. Many of the honors presented to members of Chivalric Orders are decorative and do not represent battles. It is through these types of Orders that we acquire notions such as knighthoods and dames. This is a way to mark an individual as a high-ranking member of society, even without having royal blood. Other major Chivalric Orders still in existence today are the Order of the Golden Fleece (founded in 1430), and the Order of the Gold Lion of the House of Nassau (founded in 1852). Every Chivalric Order has different goals, but they all share the same common foundations of Catholicism and chivalry.

Additionally, there is a strong presence of the Knights of Malta in the United States with many influential American citizens as members. John Dunlap worked as a New York City based attorney and was made partner with Dunnington, Bartholow & Miller LLP law firm in 1993. From there he was a legal advisor for the Permanent Observer of the Holy See to the United Nations. In 1996, Dunlap became a Knight of Magistral Grace and then took his perpetual vows in 2008. In 2022, Pope Francis created a massive change to the Knights of Malta by ending the noble family requirement to be the Grand Master of the Order. That same year, Dunlap became not only the first American but also the first person in history without nobility to become the Grand Master. Dunlap oversees the entire organization and their work. According to the Knights of Malta's US website in 2025, they currently have 30 designated office areas and collectively produce over 40,000 volunteer hours annually.

The Knights of Malta carry weight that is even greater than their volunteer service. They wield influence and power. I want to stress that influence and power are not negative. Nothing could ever be done if we did not have influential people and groups in the world. But what is intriguing here is that most people do not know the type of power that the Knights of Malta carries. Current and former members of the Central Intelligence Agency, US politicians, as well as other foreign intelligence agents and politicians, are members.[4] This is due in part to why their websites proudly post meetings they have with Presidents and Prime Ministers on a regular basis. Major organizations, whether a secret society or a Chivalric Order, tend to have impressive individuals as members, which in turn means connections to government power. It is not a conspiratorial matter of *pulling*

4. Lebedev, "Caped crusaders: What really goes on at the Knights of Malta's secretive headquarters?," lines 7–16.

the strings. But it is a matter of influence being essential for any properly functioning society. I have spoken directly with members of the Knights of Malta, and it is apparent that they are most proud of their volunteer and charitable efforts.

Diplomatic relations between the Knights of Malta and the over 100 countries they serve are for humanitarian causes. This Chivalric Order functions independently from government programs because they themselves are autonomous. They simply need a world leader's blessing to carry out their mission. Taxpayer funding does not go to the Knights of Malta either. Because of this, they generally do not require parliament or congressional approval to operate. This has served their organization well and has helped them maintain their ongoing status in society. Human connection through history is also essential. Tradition is honoring where we come from and holding it in the highest regard. The Knights of Malta's long history speaks to the past for many nations and the people that inhabit them. They do important work that positively serves society. Influence and power coming from serving the vulnerable is a noble pursuit at its finest.

CHAPTER 23

Salai

HARVARD UNIVERSITY INVITED ME to join their Office for the Arts (OFA) for the 2024–2025 school year. The invitation came as a surprise as I was not in regular contact with that department. What happened was that a previous member passed my information along to their current director, recommending me as a potential participant. I graciously, and eagerly, accepted. One of the main events that the OFA puts on every year is their Harvard Arts Festival. This event happens over several days in the spring and showcases the artwork of Harvard students, faculty, and affiliates. It not only attracts thousands of people, but also many celebrities, politicians, and other high-profile individuals. Every year the White House administration also takes part. Another event was a luncheon to celebrate the arts. During that gathering, I recommended a focus on portraiture, as this is a primary way to display people that inspire us. The suggestion was warmly received, and several portraits I had created were shown there.

Portraiture is a way to provide the viewer with a glimpse into history. In a similar fashion to the photograph, it is a time stamp. However, a picture simply locks in the exact depiction of the posing figure. Other art forms such as painting, drawing, and sculpture give grace to the artist to highlight essential aspects. Whether it is a quick sketch or a painting that takes months, portraiture allows the artist to show their subject in a way that a camera, without editing, cannot. For this reason, the concept of a muse is vital. People of all backgrounds in creative fields have used a muse to some extent. Ernest Hemingway had Adriana Ivancich as his muse, and Pablo Picasso had Lydia Corbett. It has long been speculated that Leonardo da Vinci's muse was a young man named Gian Giacomo Caprotti da Oreno. Despite what little information we have about him, he has intrigued art historians for centuries.

Gian Giacomo Caprotti da Oreno, better known simply as Salai, entered da Vinci's workshop at only the age of 10. Born in 1480, a much younger Salai was seen more as a nuisance to Leonardo da Vinci than anything else. Da Vinci even wrote disparaging remarks about him in his notebooks. Nevertheless, Salai stayed as a member of da Vinci's workshop and household for more than 25 years.[1] Initially a servant for da Vinci and his entourage, when he became older, he apprenticed as an artist in his school. We think of art today in very different terms from what it was thought of in the Renaissance. Back then if you wanted to be an artist you had to first be accepted into a workshop. The notion of a self-taught artist would have been a foreign concept to someone in da Vinci's time. An artist creating work alone did not become popularized until the era of Vincent van Gogh in the late 1800's.

Salai developed his skills as an artist over the years and remained close to da Vinci. He even made trips with Leonardo to France and Rome. However, as records of the time show, Leonardo still referred to Salai as his servant. We do not have any historical records of Leonardo da Vinci mentioning Salai as a business partner, artist, or anything of the sort. Speculation is all that we have as to why this was the case. What we do know is that Leonardo da Vinci and Salai had romantic involvements with one another. A piece of evidence for this includes the homoerotically charged art both made. These paintings and drawings were explicit, such as the genitals with legs mentioned earlier. There was little that Salai and da Vinci wrote about regarding their personal lives. But through their art, we can clearly see that their relationship involved intimacy.

Towards the end of Leonardo da Vinci's life, Salai worked at da Vinci's vineyard in Milan, where Salai's father had worked before. Upon his death, Salai inherited half of da Vinci's vineyard.[2] Leonardo himself received the vineyard as a gift from Ludovico Maria Sforza in 1498 as a kind gesture for

---

1. Stern, *Queers in History: The comprehensive encyclopedia of historical gays, lesbians, and bisexuals*, 276.

2. Rui, "Santa Maria delle Grazie," line 6.

the beautiful artwork he had been making.[3] A few years after da Vinci passed away, Salai married Bianca Coldirodi d'Annono in 1523.[4] Their marriage was unfortunately short-lived as Salai was killed the following year, most likely from a crossbow duel.[5] While we do not know much about the life of Salai, we know that he and da Vinci were important to each other. We also know that Salai went from being a troublemaker with little potential for his future to being an accomplished artist. His artwork was not only well received in his lifetime but is still sought after in the present day.

Salai's life offers a unique perspective on the Renaissance and helps us to better understand the life of Leonardo da Vinci. While Salai's artistic achievements may not match Leonardo's, his role as apprentice, companion, and lover provides a fascinating glimpse into the relationships and dynamics of da Vinci. He was a complex man and deciphering who he was is made harder by lack of documentation. However, the little information that we do have about Salai is enough to piece together a picture. Today many people view Salai as being a muse for Leonardo da Vinci. Many art historians, such as Carlo Pedretti and others, also believe Salai to have been the model for da Vinci's *Saint John the Baptist* painting. Furthermore, they attribute other paintings by da Vinci and other artists to Salai being their muse. This only adds to the mystery of who this man was.

Martin Kemp is a leading da Vinci scholar and I have had the pleasure of speaking with him several times. In one of our recent conversations, I asked Kemp about Salai being a model for the *Saint John the Baptist* painting. His response truly shocked me when he said that no one truly knows who the model for that painting was. Kemp further added that there is no worthy evidence as to what Salai looked like. Could he be incorrect? Surely, he must be mistaken. After all, this painting, and many other works, are attributed to Salai having been the model for it. But Martin Kemp is correct. We have no idea what Salai looked like. There is nothing in da Vinci's notebooks, or a single document from his time that explicitly states Salai was the model for these works. No documentation calls out any unique features he had either. The only reason why some people believe Salai to have been the model for these works is because da Vinci preferred men with curly hair. Some scholars mistakenly attribute this to Salai; however,

3. Beltrami, *Vigna di Leonardo da Vinci*, 41–42.

4. Farago, *Leonardo's Art: Twentieth-century connoisseurship and iconographic studies. Leonardo's Projects from 1500–1519. Vol. 3, 397.*

5. Calvi, *Contributi alla biografia di Leonardo da Vinci: Periodo Sforzesco*, 472–473.

this was a well-known preference of Leonardo's long before Salai ever came into the picture.[6]

Not having credible documentation for Salai's appearance is an example of how evidence can be manipulated. The line between fact and fiction is easily blurred, especially when a leading scholar perceives it as truth. Salai very well could be the model for the *Saint John the Baptist*. But the issue is that as of now, we do not have any evidence to support this claim. Just because something has been repeated perpetually does not make it true. It also does not make the *Saint John the Baptist* painting any less interesting. Whether Salai was the model for it or not, he still has a strong connection to the artwork. In 1520, one year after the death of Leonardo, Salai is thought to be the painter of another version of John the Baptist. This painting is almost identical in appearance to the da Vinci version. The left hand pointed to his chest, the right index finger pointed towards Heaven, the exposed body, and, of course, the curly hair. Leonardo da Vinci's *Saint John the Baptist* captures the hearts and minds of those who encounter it. His associates connected with da Vinci through his work of *Saint John the Baptist* even after his death.

6. Kemp, "Martin Kemp on the Prado Mona Lisa," lines 11–13.

CHAPTER 24

Bloodline

THE QUESTION OF JESUS having been married with children has been around for quite a while. The canonical gospels mention several times the importance of Mary Magdalene, and she is regularly placed at the beginning of lists of names, further highlighting her status. There is also the cultural norm aspect regarding Jesus. If he had come to this world as a human, then it would have been strange for him not to have married as most rabbis were. Furthermore, the Gnostic Gospels stress how close Jesus and Mary Magdalene were to one another. These ideas have been further popularized by various modern books such as *The Woman with the Alabaster Jar* and *The Holy Blood and the Holy Grail*. While there is no hard proof for this theory, the question is still an intriguing one.

Proponents of the Jesus Bloodline Theory point to the Kilmore Church in Scotland. Inside this church is a stained-glass window of Jesus Christ embracing a visually pregnant woman. It was made in 1906 by Stephen Adam and not much more is known beyond this. Below the image is an inscription from Luke 10:42 which reads, *Mary hath chosen that good part which shall not be taken away from her*. Those that view this work as a clue to a Jesus bloodline have failed to understand a crucial piece. The woman in the window is not Mary Magdalene, but Mary of Bethany, a different follower of Christ. In 591, Pope Gregory the Great tried to merge all *Mary* figures, other than Mother Mary, into one person. This issue has since been disentangled; however, speculators still suggest that Mary Magdalene is the one mentioned in Luke 10:42. But what about the woman in the image being pregnant? Well, that part is the remaining mystery.

Another location that has fueled speculation of a Jesus bloodline is the Rosslyn Chapel. There are many symbols throughout this place, many of which are carved right into its walls. Cryptologists have been unable to solve many of them which adds to the speculation of it being a location that holds the secret bloodline of Christ. Their reasoning suggests that many of these symbols refer to the Knights Templar, who were dissolved more than 130 years before the construction of the Rosslyn Chapel. Their theory of a Jesus bloodline states that some members of the Knights Templar carried on a secret duty protecting this secret. They then refer to this as the real Holy Grail, and the Rosslyn Chapel is a place where their secret lives on. Furthermore, they believe that throughout history there have been various leaders protecting this holy secret, and Leonardo da Vinci is one of them. Of course, there are no historical documents or other evidence that proves any of this. Nevertheless, the legend lives on, and people have devoted their lives to prove it.

The history of early Christianity was messy, violent, and discordant. Christian scholars place Jesus' crucifixion somewhere around the year 33, however, the first standardized translation and compilation of the Bible was not put together until 405. The roughly 372 years between the crucifixion and the first Bible was a time of religious turmoil among the earliest followers of Christ. Early Christians operated off a sporadic blend of verbal accounts and copies of various gospels. The Christianity that we have today has been fine-tuned over several thousand years, but the early Christians did not have this luxury. Most of Christianity's finest thinkers such as Thomas Aquinas (1225–1274), Blaise Pascal (1623–1662), and C.S. Lewis (1898–1963) did not exist until many hundreds of years after 405. In other words, early Christians lacked the scholarly research, spiritual nuance, and polemics brought forth by men such as these. It is because of this that early Christians participated in practices that were later viewed as blasphemous. So, a question to pose among the faithful is if some of these early Christians are guilty of heresy. Or are they absolved from their blasphemy on the grounds of ignorance?

What interests me is why certain holy texts carry authority. For example, the overwhelming majority of Christians today are dismissive of the Gnostic Gospels. However, if any modern Christians existed in Egypt in the year 180, they would believe in at least one of the Gnostic Gospels.

Christians today may argue that the stories in the Gnostic Gospels are too weird to be taken seriously. However, they make this assertion while fully believing in Matthew, Mark, Luke, and John which contains stories such as turning water into wine, raising people from the dead, and a virgin woman conceiving a child. Remember, to accept one doctrine of miracles means you cannot refute other doctrines of supernatural phenomena.

The Gnostic Gospels helped to shape Christianity as we know it today for the simple fact that they were rejected from the official canon. Early Christians believed these Gnostic Gospels in addition to the holy texts in the New Testament. Many Gnostic Gospels were written during the same time as Matthew, Mark, Luke, and John and they carry a deep oral tradition like the canonical gospels do. Gnostic Gospels were challenged and debated among early Christians, just as other books in the Bible were. It forced church leaders to face the nuances regarding their religious texts and made them refine their theology. The Gnostic Gospels made early, mainstream Christian leaders state what they were not, which in turn clarified what they were. One of the ways early Christians were forced into crafting a coherent message was through baptism. The Gnostic Gospels stressed the Five Seals, a more complex version of baptism, while other early Christians refined it to a simple washing of holy water with prayer.

But how might da Vinci's painting of John the Baptist turn out differently if some of the Gnostic Gospels were included in the Bible? In the Gnostic Gospel of The Life of John the Baptist, his severed head floated around the world preaching God's Word. If this were in the Bible would da Vinci alter the painting to be a more macabre, gruesome depiction, rather than a sexy ghost-human? There is also the Gospel of the Nazarenes where Christ was initially hesitant of being baptized by John. If this were in the Bible is it possible that Leonardo may have presented John in more of a deity-like form? What is left out of the Bible is just as important as what is included. Leonardo da Vinci utilized religious scripture, as well as historical depictions to make this painting. If the scriptures were different, then his painting would have been different.

Leonardo da Vinci was influenced by more than holy figures. He was also shaped by ancient Greek mythology, such as the story of *Leda and the Swan*. While there are varying differences in this story between ancient retellings, its crux remains the same. Zeus lusted after Leda, a former Aetolian princess who later became a Spartan queen. He then transformed himself into a swan and had sex with her. Leda then had two children, Helen and

Polydeuces, which she shared with Zeus. Some versions claim that Leda laid two eggs which the babies hatched from. Publius Ovidius Naso (43 BC-AD 17/18), known popularly as Ovid, wrote his own version of *Leda and the Swan* as well. Ovid was one of da Vinci's favorite writers and was a source of inspiration for him to create his artistic renderings of this ancient Greek story.

It is believed that da Vinci made a painting of *Leda and the Swan*, but it was later destroyed. All that exists now are preparatory drawings he made for it in his notebooks. Leonardo crafted these drawings in the years leading up to his painting of *Saint John the Baptist*. While these subjects might seem different, they carry a strikingly similar theme. John the Baptist is a central figure in Christianity who was morphed and molded into being viewed as a faithful follower of Christ who warned of the end times. Up until da Vinci's painting of him, John was depicted as frail and rugged with unkempt hair. Leda is a character in Greek mythology who bore children from a god in the form of an animal. She was typically depicted as a woman seduced or manipulated by the god-swan. Leonardo took on these figures in a unique, revolutionary way.

Da Vinci approached the subject of John the Baptist by portraying him as a sex symbol, rather than depicting him as a thin madman wandering through the wilderness. Now John the Baptist is shown as someone well-fed, mischievous, and handsome. His approach to Leda was akin to this method. These preparatory drawings represent her feminine elegance not typically found in his other sketches. In a rendering of Leda, da Vinci focuses on her intricate braids, highlighting a beautiful exquisiteness. This is similar to his focus on depicting John the Baptist's hair in an elegant manner. Another drawing has Leda kneeling with the swan-god emphasizing her womanly curves. The twist at her torso reflects the same type of twist da Vinci used for his *Saint John the Baptist*. The embrace between Leda and the swan-god is that of tenderness, not of manipulation or force. Just as he did with John the Baptist, these drawings of Leda revolutionized this ancient story.

In another drawing of Leda, he has her posing with her baby. The pose of Leda in this sketch is remarkably similar to the largest drawing he ever made titled, *The Virgin and Child with Saint Anne and Saint John the Baptist*. Both sets of these drawings were made around the same time as one another. The Leda drawing was made around 1504, while the drawings of Christian figures are believed to have been made from either 1499–1500 or

1506–1508. Furthermore, the figures in these drawings look similar. The chubby infant John the Baptist is almost identical to the infant in the Leda drawing. The influence of John the Baptist did not remain as a stagnate, sole impression upon Leonardo. Instead, it acted as an impetus for further creativity.

Leonardo da Vinci's depictions of his *Leda and the Swan* drawings are synonymous with his painting *Saint John the Baptist*. He uses both Leda and John to represent erotic, contentious desire that pushes the limits of attraction. Da Vinci reenvisioned how people could perceive these figures. There were also other focuses that Leonardo had during this period. Around the same time as his drawings for *Leda and the Swan* and his *The Virgin and Child with Saint Anne and Saint John the Baptist*, Leonardo was designing water hydraulics. So not only did these drawings reference John the Baptist, but he was also working on a major project involving water, the element John used for baptisms. Leonardo da Vinci challenged the constraints of creative norms and ventured into a new territory of artistic exploration.

Tales of Jesus Christ having been married with children is an intriguing legend. Gnostic Gospels, canonical gospels, and other historical sources do seem to provide clues to make this a plausible leap. However, there is no hard proof that allows for this assumption to be accepted as fact. The evidence that we do have shows that Jesus never had children, thus there is no valid reason to suggest a holy bloodline. What we can demonstrate is not only that Jesus never married and had children, but neither did John the Baptist or Leonardo da Vinci. Much focus has been placed on the plausibility of Christ having children, but that rigorous question has never been laid at the feet of John the Baptist or da Vinci. While no evidence exists for any of them establishing a bloodline, it is a conceivable thought. Who knows, maybe there are descendants of da Vinci, John the Baptist, and Jesus Christ walking among us today.

CHAPTER 25

Context and Reasoning

NOT MUCH IS KNOWN about Jesus Christ's childhood. The traditionally accepted gospels mention his birth story and when he taught in the temple as a child as told in Luke 2:41–52. However, the Gnostic Infancy Gospel of Thomas, not to be confused with the Gnostic Gospel of Thomas, also talks about his childhood. Its first known quotation comes from Irenaeus of Lyon, who was writing to criticize the text. That written quotation occurred more than 200 years before the first unified translation and compilation of the Bible. This means that this Gnostic Gospel is much older than Irenaeus of Lyon's criticism of it. Whether the Infancy Gospel of Thomas is true is not the right question to debate. One of the reasons why debating it is futile is because ultimately all miracles are spurious. Accepting miracles from one religion, while refusing to believe in the validity of miracles from other faiths, shows a remarkable bias.

Holy texts have the objective of convincing people to believe in their god. Miracles and other phenomena are found throughout religious texts in efforts to prove that their faith is the right one. The so-called miracles performed by Jesus were exaggerated over the course of the almost 400 years between his death and Saint Jerome's Vulgate. His miraculous acts at the time could easily have been a sleight of hand. As Robert M. Price has pointed out, when Jesus walked on water he could have been essentially on shore and his disciples did not know how close to land they were due to the storm. Or the miraculous loaves and fish story where the food never ran out. What is more plausible, that the baskets of food never emptied, or that a stockpile of food was continuously brought out from the cave by stealthy disciples?[1] Miracles are tools used in religious works in an attempt to attract followers.

The Gnostic Infancy Gospel of Thomas, which contains many miracles, portrays Jesus as a mischievous child. One of the miracles this young Jesus performs is when Joseph rebukes him for playing with clay on the Sabbath. A frustrated 5-year-old Jesus clapped his hands, and the clay turned into a dozen sparrows, and they all flew away. Another story was when the young Jesus was playing on a roof with friends and one of them fell and died. The parents of the village accused a rattled Jesus of killing the kid. So, to prove his innocence, Jesus raised his friend from the dead, and his friend told the adults that Jesus did not push him. Upon proving his innocence, Jesus then demanded his friend *Fall asleep* in which he returned to his death.

People of any religion can wonder what their prophet was like as a child. Some faiths account for this, while others only focus on the prophet's ministry as an adult. This Gnostic Gospel attempts to fill in these blanks for faithful Christians wanting to know what the Son of God was like when he was young. Many Christians later on wondered about what John the Baptist was like in his youth as well. However, the Bible and the Gnostic Gospels do not talk much about his childhood either. Similarly, we do not know much about Leonardo da Vinci's childhood. Having been born as an illegitimate child during a period where extensive documentation on people was not widespread, many blanks remain. It was not until later in da Vinci's life that others began writing about him because by then he had achieved prominent status in society. But as an unknown child in a quaint town, there wouldn't have been much to write about.

In July 2024 I received a much-anticipated email saying that my research on the da Vinci painting, *Saint John the Baptist*, had been accepted. Upon acceptance it took around 10 months of editing and revisions before being published. While it takes an extraordinary amount of work to conduct proper research, it is all worth it when it is published by a journal. Sifting through ancient documents, none of which were in English, made the research even more challenging. However, this is essential work because there is still much more to be uncovered about Leonardo da Vinci. Art historians have only scratched the surface with him. Conducting original

1. Price, *Case Against the Case for Christ: A New Testament Scholar Refutes Lee Strobel*, 208.

research and having it published in a scholarly journal helps to elevate our understanding of da Vinci. My research was published in The Other Journal, an academic publication at The Seattle School of Theology & Psychology.

My research paper focused solely on Leonardo da Vinci's final painting of his life, *Saint John the Baptist*. Da Vinci had always been surrounded by the influence of John the Baptist. Hundreds of years before his birth, the Crusades created a lasting impact. The Knights Templar and the accusations involving John the Baptist further cemented his influence. Then the Knights Hospitaller of Saint John the Baptist took over the Knights Templar's funding and property. Leonardo's favorite written work, *Divine Comedy* by Dante Alighieri features these knighthoods as well as John the Baptist as a prominent character. Leonardo's friendship with Charles II d'Amboise, whose uncle was the Grand Master of the Knights Hospitaller of Saint John the Baptist, further strengthens this connection. This deep history and influence penetrated the heart and mind of Leonardo.

John the Baptist was also a central figure in Florence. He was featured on their currency, and he was the city's patron saint. Furthermore, the Florence Baptistery is mentioned in Dante's *Divine Comedy*. Not only was Dante himself baptized there, but it was also the location where da Vinci helped Rustici design his John the Baptist statues. Da Vinci survived the Plague in Milan and attempted to create a new city to prevent future plagues. This forced him to reflect on his mortality. Since Leonardo was a Catholic, the belief in baptism through Holy Water guaranteed his salvation, whether the Plague reached him or not. Leonardo also lived through the Age of Discovery where brave explorers such as Christopher Columbus discovered unknown parts of the globe. This discovery of the *beyond* acted as a metaphor for the afterlife for many people, including da Vinci. His *Saint John the Baptist* painting suggests what this spiritual *beyond* is.

Leonardo da Vinci also lived for a time at Santissima Annunziata. Here he was surrounded by Catholic artwork, including various depictions of John the Baptist. A notable example is the painting by Alessio Baldovinetti. Inspiration for depicting John was seen at every turn. It was during Leonardo's time at Santissima Annunziata that he made the largest drawing of his life, *The Virgin and Child with Saint Anne and Saint John the Baptist*. Da Vinci created many other paintings and drawings that featured John the Baptist as well. Around the time of completing *Saint John the Baptist*, da Vinci began his series of apocalyptic drawings. These sketches depicted major catastrophes, and only those faithfully baptized in the name of Christ, escape. The influence of John the Baptist and the act of baptism is a major recurring theme in these apocalyptic drawings. These sketches are housed in the Royal Trust Collection of England (RTC). The RTC's official stance on these drawings is that Leonardo made them during a period in which death was at the forefront of his mind.[2]

I spoke with Carmen Bambach, another leading da Vinci scholar, and she believes this painting was created for private devotion. This was a rather common request and is in alignment with the primary sources at our disposal. Other art historians specify the ambiguity between the body and spirit in the painting.[3] Furthermore, there is a prominent homoerotic element to it which is heavily backed by da Vinci's personal life. I do not dispute any of these assessments. However, previous scholarship has left out the critical question of why he depicted John the Baptist in this manner? After adding in the previously mentioned pieces of historical evidence for proper context, the answer becomes simple. Leonardo da Vinci's painting, *Saint John the Baptist*, is a reflection on death.

Leonardo da Vinci lived in an age of intensive Christendom and the Vatican was at the head. Kingdoms, as well as powerful families like the Medicis, further implemented the Vatican's power. Everywhere da Vinci went he was inundated with religious iconography and religious influences. Adding to the fact that he was Catholic and religiously-based commissions were prevalent, it makes sense why Leonardo made religious artwork. John the Baptist has always been an incredibly popular biblical character. His teachings on following God, waiting for the Messiah, and baptism reigned supreme in the High Renaissance. It can be hard to imagine a single person having such a dominant influence over us today. However, this was the case for the people living in the High Renaissance with John the Baptist. This prophet represents death and salvation, which was at the forefront of da Vinci's mind when he made the painting.

The context of Leonardo's *Saint John the Baptist* is that it reflects nearly 1,500 years of evolving views on the prophet by the time it was painted. Canonical and Gnostic Gospels formulated the myth and legend of this figure who brought forth the power of baptism. Through this sacrament, the followers of Christ could be washed of the sins of Adam and Eve to worship their God in Paradise. John the Baptist was brought to even further

2. Royal Trust Collection, "Apocalyptic scenes, with notes c.1517–18," lines 8–11.

3. Barolsky, *Leonardo Da Vinci, Selected Scholarship: Leonardo's projects, c. 1500–1519*, 394.

prominence from the Crusades and Chivalric Orders. In the following centuries, popular figures such as Dante Alighieri and Domenico Cavalca further popularized John the Baptist through their writings. All of this is then compiled with the influence of John in the cities where da Vinci lived.

The reason behind the painting is that Leonardo da Vinci used the symbolism of this prophet as a reflection on his own life. John the Baptist had previously been depicted by other artists as this malnourished, wild man who wandered through the wilderness preaching the end times. Da Vinci had to think of a way to portray The Baptist that honors his religious tradition, while also using the painting as a mirror. So, Leonardo added the traditional objects of the subject being dressed in fur and holding a reed cross to signify this was John the Baptist. But he added curly hair, a preference da Vinci had for men, as well as a beautiful face and well-built body. Leonardo da Vinci was not only influenced by John the Baptist everywhere he went, but he also saw much of himself in this prophet. *Saint John the Baptist* reflects who da Vinci believed himself to be: A revolutionary, thought-provoking innovator. A beautiful man whose earthly ambitions and desires will transcend to the outer realms of our human understanding of the cosmos. This painting is a reflection on his life and what was to come next.

In Leonardo da Vinci's Codex Atlanticus folio 680r, he wrote *quando io credero imparare a vivere, e io imparero a morire.* This translates to mean, *While I thought I was learning how to live, I have been learning how to die.* We don't know if Leonardo came up with this line on his own, or if he wrote it down upon hearing it from someone else. All that we know is that he found it important enough to keep in his records. Written in his classic mirror writing, it clarifies his psyche. Leonardo was acutely aware that our time on earth is limited and that we have the opportunity to make the most out of it. Fleeting moments abandon us before we even have the chance to wonder where it all went. Leonardo da Vinci's life was a race against a clock. A clock which he did not know when it was to run out.

CHAPTER 26

Everlasting Presence

DAPHNE CARUANA GALIZIA WAS a journalist who sought to expose corruption. Galizia followed the money, followed actions, and immediately wrote about it. Some people saw her work as sensational. Maybe some of it was. Others saw her as teetering on the edge of paranoia. Maybe she was. But her quickly written blogs were meant to push the message out promptly. Her potential paranoia also proved correct due to being killed in a car bomb in 2017. The killing of Daphne Galizia speaks loudly for the citizens of Malta in which some of their citizens walk the tightrope of paranoia themselves. Sure, many of their claims are outlandish. But those peculiar thoughts come from a place of harsh reality. A reality of open corruption where the ones that design the rules are the ones allowed to break them. Galizia is an example of what happens when someone writes about it.

With corruption plaguing Malta, many of its citizens seek to place blame on what they deem to be secretive, formidable organizations. The island's proximity to Sicily has bolstered the people's view on corruption. Shouts of *Mafia* towards politicians speak to the historical and geographical ties to Sicily as if there is a direct connection between them. Citizens verbally hurling *Opus Dei* at people of power attempts to paint them as a cabal of devil worshippers. Then there are the allegations of individuals involved in corruption as being Freemasons. Some may be Freemasons; others may have some distant connection to Freemasonry. But by and large, there is no connection at all. The main reason for these accusations is that these people come from a place of helplessness. They see the corruption around them. They see the murders. They crave answers. For many people, a junk theory provides them with more comfort than not having a theory.

Opus Dei was not involved in the death of Daphne Galizia as there is no evidence. If there is a connection, then evidence has yet to emerge. However, their perceived secretive nature, as well as a constant stream of other, unrelated controversies, makes them a target. The reality is that members of Opus Dei have outright condemned her killing. The Freemasons were also not involved in her murder. Just as with Opus Dei, evidence does not show any involvement between Freemasonry and Daphne's death. They even offered services and resources to assist the authorities in finding the perpetrators. As far as the mafia goes, that is a matter of what your definition of *mafia* is. I take the traditional approach of it meaning a family-based criminal organization with military-style ranks. By this definition, a *mafia* does not seem to be involved either. Many questions about Daphne's death remain, and this only adds to the blurred lines between fiction and reality.

What does remain out in the open is the Sovereign Military Hospitaller Order of Saint John the Baptist of Jerusalem. Today they are most known as the Knights of Malta. This chivalric order goes back 1,000 years with a direct line traveling to the present day. Their worldwide presence as a noble charitable organization has increased their status and influence. Their impact is particularly felt in Malta, a nation they once ruled hundreds of years ago. For the Maltese people, who are mostly Catholic, the Knights of Malta represent their history. They are not only overseen by the Pope himself but have direct connections to the highest-ranking politicians in Malta. Their influence helps to set policy and sway public opinion. The grandeur of a chivalric order should not be viewed as an unnecessary, over-the-top costume party. It is tradition. Over the centuries, this tradition has developed into total sustainability for their order. It is not a bad thing either. But it is a powerful influence, nevertheless.

While Maltese citizens angrily hurl accusations of *Opus Dei* and *Freemasonry* at people allegedly involved in corruption, they never hurl *Knights of Malta* as an insult. Of course, the Knights of Malta had nothing to do with Galizia's assassination, but neither did these other groups. And with the Knights of Malta's proximity to the people allegedly responsible for her death, it could be imagined that people would point the finger at them too. I believe the Knights of Malta have thwarted this for several reasons. Not only do they have a public presence, but they also carry deep, historic ties to Malta. I mean, they were the rulers over this tiny European island once before. This factored in with the nation's high Catholic population, removes the urge to launch unfounded accusations against them. Going against the Knights of Malta would be the equivalent of going against who the Maltese citizens are as a people. The Knights of Malta may even be viewed as the one faction Maltese citizens are not angry with.

As time went on after the assassination of Daphne Galizia, Maltese citizens grew angrier. Paranoid suspicions now hold a place in reality. Details emerged about the car bomb, and it became clear that she was not given government protection. Speculation from this only grew. From this came alleged links between the assassination and the government of the Republic of Malta.[1] The country then plummeted into political turmoil. Years of speculation and corruption reached a boiling point that brought about the 2019 Maltese Protests. Thousands of people took to the streets demanding a new government. Their anger only grew when reports came out during the protests of intimidation tactics that the Maltese government used against journalists.[2] Truth and falsehoods continued to be blurred during this time. Just as with researching da Vinci, it can be challenging to separate fact from fiction with the Galizia assassination.

Daphne Galizia wrote about lavish gifts and cash being sent from the presidential family of Azerbaijan directly to Malta's Prime Minister Joseph Muscat, his family, and a prostitution ring in London.[3] This was far from the only scandals Galizia wrote about regarding the Maltese government. Stemming from the protests, a public inquiry found that the government of Malta was responsible for the death of Daphne Galizia. A 437-page report stated that government leaders *created an atmosphere of impunity, generated by the highest echelons.*[4] Galizia was a high-profile investigative journalist who did not receive necessary protection. The allegation that comes from this is that she wrote critically about the very people responsible for her safety. Public perception is that the government intentionally failed her.

1. Rankin, "Suspect in Daphne Caruana Galizia murder says he got tipoffs from official," lines 1–19.

2. Farrugia, "International journalism groups condemn 'intimidation' of reporters in Malta," lines 1–10.

3. Jansson, "This has happened: The murder of Maltese journalist Daphne Caruana Galizia," lines 1–8.

4. BBC, "Daphne Caruana Galizia: Malta responsible for journalist death—inquiry," lines 1–23.

What ultimately came from this was a wave of resignations from the highest powers in Malta.

Keith Schembri, Chief of Staff to Prime Minister Joseph Muscat, resigned from his post in November 2019 about the assassination of Galizia. He was then promptly arrested by the police.[5] Schembri was later released. It is eerie to find the last post Galizia published on her blog, *Running Commentary*, is titled *That crook Schembri was in court today, pleading that he is not a crook*. Additionally, Prime Minister Joseph Muscat pardoned an alleged middleman of the murder in exchange for information which led to further public distrust. From there, Tourism Minister Konrad Mizzi and Economy Minister Chris Cardona resigned over alleged corruption and connections to the attack. The alleged mastermind behind the attack, Yorgen Fenech, owner of 17 Black, maintains his innocence. What does not help his case is that Daphne Galizia wrote about Fenech's alleged corruption involving the Maltese government.[6] Everyone mentioned here has maintained their innocence and stated they had zero involvement in her death.

The biggest resignation came from Prime Minister Joseph Muscat himself. In December 2019, Muscat announced his resignation beginning in the upcoming year of 2020.[7] Former Prime Minister Joseph Muscat has not been formally charged, let alone convicted, for the death of Galizia. However, his failure to act against Keith Schembri and Konrad Mizzi for their alleged involvement led to a mess of accusations.[8] Following a new election, Robert Abela became the Prime Minister of Malta. These resignations, however, did not signal the end of corruption. In March 2024, Prime Minister Robert Abela faced alleged banking controversies. Supposedly, Abela had suspicious transactions with no separation between his own personal, political, and business finances.[9] Furthermore, Chris Fearne resigned as Deputy Prime Minister of Malta in October 2024 over allegations of misappropriation and fraud regarding a healthcare scheme.[10]

5. BBC, "Malta Caruana murder: Resignations spark government crisis,"

6. BBC, "Malta Caruana murder: Resignations spark government crisis," lines 1–28.

7. Grech, "Muscat to step down as Prime Minister after January 12," lines 1–11.

8. Kirchgaessner, "How Joseph Muscat's glittering political career lost its lustre," lines 32–37.

9. Magri, "'Now we understand why Abela did not want the 'unexplained wealth order': Grech," lines 1–11.

10. Iribarren, "Malta loses its commissioner nominee over hospital corruption scandal," lines 1–14.

Let's summarize these accusations. George and Alfred Degiorgio have been sentenced for killing Galizia with a car bomb. Yorgen Fenech is still awaiting charges and a trial for his company 17 Black, connections to Konrad Mizzi and Keith Schembri, as well as potentially orchestrating the assassination. Former Chief of Staff, Keith Schembri, is awaiting further potential charges regarding money laundering, corruption, and Galizia's death. Konrad Mizzi is facing money laundering charges, as well as his connections to Schembri. There are even more individuals caught on this web. Brian Tonna and Karl Cinni are awaiting criminal charges because of ties to 17 Black and money laundering.[11] Galizia wrote cryptically about 17 Black and their alleged involvement with corruption involving politicians. She never discovered who its owner was because she was killed in a car bomb eight months after its publication.[12] Former Prime Minister Joseph Muscat resigned from his position and has since faced charges of money laundering and corruption. He maintains his innocence. Muscat has further stated that these charges stem from a place of animosity over his handling of the Galizia assassination.[13]

The Knights of Malta's access to government leaders is profound. On the US delegation of the Knights of Malta's website, on their gallery page, is an official photograph of them with former Prime Minister Joseph Muscat. There was more than just a photograph that Muscat took with them too. In April 2015, the Knights of Malta met with him to discuss an African migrant crisis. They sought further cooperation between them and the government which appears to have been granted.[14] Another time Muscat publicly met with them was when he hosted the Knights to celebrate the 450th anniversary of the Great Siege of Malta. This was the historic moment when the Knights Hospitaller, now known as the Knights of Malta, held off foreign invaders. They later met privately with Muscat to discuss foreign policy.[15] Joseph Muscat is far from the only political leader with deep ties to them.

---

11. Borg, "Joseph, Keith, Konrad, Yorgen: Who's been charged with what?," lines 1–44.

12. Arnold, "Exclusive: Mystery company named by murdered Maltese journalist is linked to power station developer," lines 1–8.

13. Rankin, "Malta's former prime minister charged with corruption over hospital scandal," 1–7.

14. Malta, "Historical Legacy, Migration and Fort St. Angelo discussed during the Grand Master's State Visit to the Republic of Malta," lines 6–17.

15. Malta, "Great Siege of Malta 450 years ago," lines 1–20.

Prime Minister Robert Abela's father, George Abela, was the President of Malta and had connections to the knighthood. Right after George Abela became the newly elected leader, one of his first official meetings was with them. During this meeting, they discussed international humanitarian aid, as well as the importance of their history. The Knights of Malta then threw a large dinner party in George Abela's honor.[16] In 2011, the Knights of Malta celebrated their 53rd international pilgrimage. Their guest of honor was, again, George Abela. He helped to host this massive event along with the Knight's Grand Master.[17] While in office, George Abela further supported various charitable efforts by them, which further increased their status.

George Abela's son, Robert, is now the Prime Minister of Malta after replacing Joseph Muscat. Robert also has strong connections to the Knights. He was a commanding presence at the funeral of Grand Master Father Matthew Festing.[18] Robert Abela attended many ceremonies hosted by the Knights of Malta, which further highlights their importance. One of these ceremonies was the 10th Anniversary of the Episcopal Ordination at St John's Co-Cathedral in Valletta.[19] In December 2023, shortly before the 60th Anniversary of the independence of Malta, Robert met with the archbishop, as well as members of the Knights of Malta, to discuss the occasion.[20] None of this is controversial as dignitaries meet with political leaders every single day. But what is important to note is the power and influence that the Knights of Malta carry. The highest government leaders of Malta meet with them at their behest. Recent reports state that Prime Minister Robert Abela is working with the Knights of Malta for a potential streaming series about the Knights Hospitaller. This project is being created by Hollywood actor and filmmaker, Mel Gibson.[21]

The genesis of the Knights of Malta is their adoration of Saint John the Baptist. This revolutionary, apocalyptic preacher who baptized Christ created an everlasting presence in the world. This knighthood dedicated their entire cause to him, which further expanded the prophet's reach. We can

16. Malta, "Historic ties and shared projects: visit of Maltese (P)resident George Abela," lines 1–7.

17. Malta, "Lourdes: the 53rd International pilgrimage of the Order of Malta," lines 1–13.

18. Malta, "Funeral of Fra' Matthew Festing in Malta," lines 8–12.

19. Malta, "Archbishop's Tenth Anniversary," lines 1–4.

20. Malta, "Exchange of Greetings," lines 1–9.

21. Marie, "Mel Gibson's Upcoming Series on the Siege of Malta," lines 9–14.

see John the Baptist's influence everywhere. In literature, music, art, and so forth. He has forever remained a constant presence. The Knights of Malta carry immense influence in the world, especially in the Republic of Malta. But it is John the Baptist himself that inspires them. At every meeting with a political leader, these Knights bring their history along with them, just as they have done for centuries. Their orders come from the Vatican, but their meaning comes from Saint John the Baptist. As various Maltese politicians are accused of assassinations and other levels of corruption, the Knights of Malta remain unscathed.

Leonardo da Vinci was immersed in the influence of Saint John the Baptist throughout his entire life. This saturation further inspired the work that he created. *Saint John the Baptist* is a painting that was da Vinci's reflection on his existence and upcoming death. He was looking back on his life, and all that he had accomplished, and was thinking of what was to come. The prophet fits this question perfectly as it is through baptism that Christians believe will unlock their eternal reward with God in Heaven. Leonardo also painted him in such a way as to highlight his playful approach to life. By the time da Vinci started this painting he was an old man, no longer youthful, and nearing the other side. This painting was him reflecting on his own time on earth. Da Vinci's portrayal of John the Baptist in this revolutionary way was meant as a means of entering a new realm. The old was behind him, and the new was approaching.

There is one final discovery regarding this masterpiece. The date of creation for the *Saint John the Baptist* painting is from approximately 1513–1516. However, during its x-rays at the Louvre from 2015 to 2016, the C2RMF team found that Leonardo da Vinci continued to work on this painting up until the moment of his death in 1519.[22] Leonardo created this painting to reflect on his life and upcoming death. In the days before taking his last breath, da Vinci used his dwindling strength to still work on this painting. As he was nearing his end, he looked to his *Saint John the Baptist* painting to make it even more perfect than what it already was. Leonardo da Vinci deeply felt John the Baptist's impact. This prophet's impression was prominent not only during the Renaissance but also in our modern age. Just as there is a direct line from the Crusades to the present moment with the Knights of Malta, there is a direct line of John the Baptist in our current world.

---

22. Tarbox, "Risky Business of Restoring Leonardos," lines 54–57.

Da Vinci scholars have correctly assessed the *Saint John the Baptist* painting by highlighting its sfumato and chiaroscuro techniques. They have also done an incredible job of calling out its ambiguous nature between spirit and human. However, what academics have not thoroughly done is place this painting within its appropriate context. *Saint John the Baptist* was created as da Vinci was nearing the end of his life. But it was not only Leonardo's mortality that inspired the work. It was also the circumstances that helped to shape who he became. For the same reasons we cannot ignore the Gnostic Gospels regarding early Christianity, we cannot disregard the elements that helped to shape and inspire Leonardo da Vinci. *Saint John the Baptist* is a painting that is hundreds of years in the making. It is more than a portrait. It is a prophecy. It is a time capsule. It is history. It is the ashes that we were molded from, and the dust to which we shall return. This painting is the signifier of death and the reflection of a life that was well deserved.

Bibliography

Aberth, John. *From the Brink of the Apocalypse: Confronting Famine, War, Plague and Death in the Later Middle Ages*. London: Routledge, 2010.

Acidini, Cristina. "Palazzo Vecchio, Sala dei Gigli." https://musefirenze.it/en/exhibits/leonardo-da-vinci-and-firenze/#:~:text=In%20Milan%2C%20Leonardo%20was%20in,at%20the%20stake%20in%201498.

Agius, Matthew. "Patrick Dalli insults Chief Justice in open court after son's drug trafficking statement deemed admissible." https://www.maltatoday.com.mt/news/court_and_police/123209/patrick_dalli_insults_chief_justice_in_open_court_after_sons_drug_trafficking_sentence_confirmed.

Ambrosini, Maria. *The Secret Archives of the Vatican*. Boston: Little, Brown, & Co, 1969.

AP. "Panama Papers: The South Pacific's role." https://web.archive.org/web/20160517051220/http://www.nzherald.co.nz/world/news/article.cfm?c_id=2&objectid=11636649.

Arnold, Tom. "Exclusive: Mystery company named by murdered Maltese journalist is linked to power station developer." https://www.reuters.com/article/world/exclusive-mystery-company-named-by-murdered-maltese-journalist-is-linked-to-pow-idUSKCN1NE18M/.

Asciak, Michael. "Daphne's Article is three years late." https://www.independent.com.mt/articles/2007-11-25/letters/daphnes-article-is-three-years-late-200131/.

———. "Good and bad people in government." https://www.pressreader.com/malta/the-malta-independent-on-sunday/20160313/281711203754233.

Assange, Julian. "Julian Assange offers €20k reward for information on Caruana Galizia murder." https://www.maltatoday.com.mt/news/national/81361/julian_assange_offers_20k_reward_for_information_on_caruana_galizia_murder.

Attwood, Margaret. "A year after her murder, where is the justice for Daphne Caruana Galizia?." https://www.theguardian.com/commentisfree/2018/oct/16/murder-justice-daphne-caruana-galizia-malta.

Babcock, Emily. *A History of Deeds Done Beyond the Sea: William of Tyre*. New York: Columbia University Press, 1943.

Balfour, Patrick. *The Ottoman Centuries: The Rise and Fall of the Turkish Empire*. New York: Morrow, 1979.

Balzan, Jurgen. "Curia shoots down blogger's 'false' claims on Alfred Sant's annulment." https://newsbook.com.mt/en/curia-shoots-down-bloggers-false-claims-on-alfred-sants-annulment/.

———. "Jailed Daphne murderer allowed to attend family baptism party." https://newsbook.com.mt/en/jailed-daphne-murderer-allowed-to-attend-family-baptism-party/.

Barber, Malcom. *The Trial of the Templars*. New York: Cambridge University Press, 1993.

Baring, Maurice. *Thoughts on Art and Life by Leonardo da Vinci*. Boston: Merrymount, 1906.

Barolsky, Paul. *Leonardo Da Vinci, Selected Scholarship: Leonardo's projects, c. 1500–1519*. Oxfordshire: Taylor & Francis, 1999.

BBC. "Daphne Caruana Galizia: Malta responsible for journalist death—inquiry." https://www.bbc.com/news/world-europe-58012903.

———. "Malta businessman held on yacht in journalist murder probe." https://www.bbc.com/news/world-europe-50485721.

———. "Malta Caruana murder: Resignations spark government crisis." https://www.bbc.com/news/world-europe-50556578.

Beltrami, Luca. *La Vigna di Leonardo da Vinci*. Milan: Allegretta, 1920.

Berzock, Kathleen. "Caravans of Gold, Fragments in Time." https://caravans.library.northwestern.edu/works/29/.

Bil-Malti, Aqra. "Yorgen Fenech says he should be granted bail because he has been in jail for 30 months." https://tvmnews.mt/en/news/yorgen-fenech-says-he-should-be-granted-bail-because-he-has-been-in-jail-for-30-months/.

Blumenthal, Betsy. "13 Things You Didn't Know About the Louvre." https://www.cntraveler.com/story/things-you-didnt-know-about-the-louvre-museum.

Bonello, Giovanni. *Bontadino de Bontadini—The Murder of the First Baroque Architect in Malta*. Valletta: Fondazzjoni Patrimonju Malti, 2000.

Bonnici, Julian. "Daphne Caruana Galizia assassination: A week and a crime like no other." https://www.independent.com.mt/articles/2017–10-22/local-news/Daphne-Caruana-Galizia-assassination-A-week-and-a-crime-like-no-other-6736180522.

———. "Daphne Caruana Galizia's libel suits can still continue—lawyer Joseph Zammit Maempel." https://www.independent.com.mt/articles/2017–10-21/local-news/Daphne-Caruana-Galizia-s-libel-suits-can-still-continue-lawyer-Joseph-Zammit-Maempel-6736180470.

Borg, Jacob. "Joseph, Keith, Konrad, Yorgen: Who's been charged with what?" https://timesofmalta.com/article/joseph-keith-konrad-yorgen-who-charged-what.1103320.

Borg, Neville. "90% Caucasian, 83% Roman Catholic: Malta census statistics released." https://timesofmalta.com/article/90-caucasian-83-roman-catholic-malta-census-statistics-released.1014045.

Brincat, Edwina. "Daphne hitman Vince Muscat gets seven-month sentence for biting prisoner." https://timesofmalta.com/article/daphne-hitman-vince-muscat-gets-seven-month-sentence-biting-prisoner.1013355.

Brinkhof, Tim. "Ken Burns on what we get wrong about Leonardo da Vinci." https://bigthink.com/high-culture/da-vinci-documentary/.

Britannica, The Editors of Encyclopedia. "Alessio Baldovinetti." https://www.britannica.com/biography/Alessio-Baldovinetti.

———. "Arianism." https://www.britannica.com/topic/Arianism.

———. "Fra Bartolommeo." https://www.britannica.com/biography/Leonardo-da-Vinci/Second-Florentine-period-1500–08.

Burke, Tony. "More Christian Apocrypha Updates 13: Life of John the Baptist by Serapion." https://www.apocryphicity.ca/2014/10/10/more-christian-apocrypha-updates-13-life-of-john-the-baptist-by-serapion/.

Calafato, Trevor. "Homicide Trends in Malta from 1970–2018: First Findings." https://www.um.edu.mt/library/oar/bitstream/123456789/61392/1/Homicide_trends_in_Malta_from_1970_2018_first_findings_2018.pdf.

Calleja, Claudia. "The bomber who killed Karin Grech 'was a loner.'" https://www.timesofmalta.com/article/The-bomber-who-killed-Karin-Grech-was-a-loner-.400304.

Calvi, Gerolamo. *Contributi alla biografia di Leonardo da Vinci: Periodo Sforzesco*. Milan: Casa Editrice L.F. Cogliati, 1916.

Carbonell, Bettina. *Carbonell Museum Studies: An Anthology of Contexts*. Hoboken: Wiley, 2003.

Castle, Tim. "Columbus debunker sets sights on Leonardo da Vinci." https://www.abc.net.au/news/2008-07-29/da-vinci-drawings-from-chinese-originals-author/456386.

Chaaraoui, Layal. "A Conversation with Dr. Carol Swain." https://harvardindependent.com/a-conversation-with-dr-carol-swain/.

Chaumeil, Jean-Luc. *La Table d'Isis ou Le Secret de la Lumière, Editions Guy Trédaniel*. Paris: Les Éditions Trédaniel, 1994.

Cheshire, Lee. "Louvre retains its place as the most-visited art museum in the world." https://www.theartnewspaper.com/2023/03/27/louvre-retains-its-place-as-the-most-visited-art-museum-in-the-world.

Craven, Jackie. "Leonardo's Last Years." https://www.thoughtco.com/leonardos-last-years-177241.

Dalby, Douglas. "Panama Papers helps recover more than $1.2 billion around the world." https://www.icij.org/investigations/panama-papers/panama-papers-helps-recover-more-than-1-2-billion-around-the-world/.

Danziger, Elon. *Fiorenza Figlia di Roma: New Light on the Baptistery of San Giovanni and the Chronology of Florentine Romanesque Architecture*. Florence: Mitteilungen des Kunsthistorischen Institutes, 2024.

Degiorgio, Stephen. *Palaces and Lodgings of the Knights of St John at Malta*. Rome: Logart Press, 2010.

Delia, Adrian. "The death of a crusading journalist rocks Malta." https://www.economist.com/europe/2017/10/21/the-death-of-a-crusading-journalist-rocks-malta.

Diamant, Jeff. "About four-in-ten U.S. adults believe humanity is 'living in the end times.'" https://www.pewresearch.org/short-reads/2022/12/08/about-four-in-ten-u-s-adults-believe-humanity-is-living-in-the-end-times/#:~:text=In%20the%20United%20States%2C%2039,living%20in%20the%20end%20times.

Earle, Peter. *Corsairs of Malta and Barbary*. London: Sidgwick & Jackson, 1970.

Edgeller, Johnathan. *Taking the Templar Habit: Rule, Initiation Ritual, and the Accusations Against the Order*. Lubbock: Texas Tech University, 2010.

Ehrman, Bart. *Heaven and Hell: A History of the Afterlife*. New York: Simon & Schuster, 2021.

———. "How Paul Persecuted the Christians." https://ehrmanblog.org/how-paul-persecuted-the-christians/.

———. *Jesus, Interrupted*. San Francisco: HarperOne, 2009.

———. *Lost Scriptures*. New York: Oxford University Press, 2003.

———. *Peter, Paul, and Mary Magdalene: The Followers of Jesus in History and Legend.* Oxford: Oxford University Press, 2006.

Farago, Claire. *Leonardo's Art: Twentieth-century connoisseurship and iconographic studies. Leonardo's Projects from 1500–1519.* Vol. 3. Oxfordshire: Taylor and Francis, 1999.

Farley, William. "Girolamo Savonarola, The Prophet of Florence." https://williampfarley. com/girolamo-savonarola-the-prophet-of-florence/#:~:text=GIROLAMO%20 SAVONAROLA%20was%20born%20in,to%20the%20Wittenberg%20church%20 door.

Farrugia, Claire. "International journalism groups condemn 'intimidation' of reporters in Malta." https://timesofmalta.com/article/international-journalism-groups-con demn-intimidation-of-reporters-in.754510.

———*Jesus, Interrupted.* New York: HarperCollins, 2009.

Fehrenbach, Frank. *Taking Flight: Leonardo's Childhood Memories.* Cambridge: Harvard University Press, 2013.

Fiore, Julia. "6 Things You Don't Know about Leonardo da Vinci." https://www.artsy.net/ article/artsy-editorial-6-things-leonardo-da-vinci.

Galizia, Daphne. "From National Geographic News." https://daphnecaruanagalizia. com/2009/04/from-national-geographic-news/.

———. "Konrad Mizzi's and Sai Mizzi Liang's Easter lunch." https://web.archive.org/ web/20180804201653/https://daphnecaruanagalizia.com/2016/02/konrad-mezzos-and-sai-mizzi-liangs-easter-lunch/.

———. "New meaning to painted tombs—with this one, even the exterior fails to impress." https://daphnecaruanagalizia.com/2014/04/new-meaning-to-painted-tombs/.

———. "So many Freemasons cluttered around Delia." https://daphnecaruanagalizia. com/2017/09/many-freemasons-cluttered-around-delia/.

Galizia, Paul. "'I knew it was a car bomb straight away': the day my mother Daphne Caruana Galizia was murdered." https://www.theguardian.com/world/2023/oct/14/ malta-killing-of-journalist-daphne-caruana-galizia-her-son-paul-looks-back.

Ganado, Philip. "Daphne Caruana Galizia. . . Malta's most controversial journalist." https://web.archive.org/web/20171017042152/https://www.timesofmalta.com/ articles/view/20171016/local/who-was-daphne-caruana-galizia.660577.

Garside, Juliette. "Man guilty of Daphne Caruana Galizia murder given 15-year sentence." https://amp.theguardian.com/world/2021/feb/23/man-accused-daphne-caruana-galizia-assassination-pleads-guilty-vincent-muscat.

Geneanet. "Charles II D'Amboise." https://gw.geneanet.org/dedee5?lang=en&n=d+amboi se&oc=0&p=charles+ii&type=fiche.

Grech, Herman. "Maltese cross most popular by far." https://web.archive.org/web /20060617005727/http://www.timesofmalta.com/core/rticle.php?id=226742.

———. "Muscat to step down as Prime Minister after January 12." https://timesofmalta. com/article/hold-muscat-expected-to-make-statement.754168.

Haensch, Stephanie. "Distinct clones of Yersinia pestis caused the black death." https:// pmc.ncbi.nlm.nih.gov/articles/PMC2951374/.

Harris, Sam. "Neural correlates of maintaining one's political beliefs in the face of counterevidence." https://www.nature.com/articles/srep39589.

Harris, Stephen. *Understanding the Bible.* Palo Alto: Mayfield, 1985.

Hassig, Ross. "El sacrificio y las guerras floridas." https://arqueologiamexicana.mx/ mexico-antiguo/el-sacrificio-y-las-guerras-floridas.

Hatfield, Rab. "Botticelli's Mystic Nativity, Savonarola and the Millennium." https://maypoleofwisdom.com/wp-content/uploads/2021/03/botticellis-mystic-nativity.pdf.

Henley, Jon. "Pope writes rare letter of condolence after murder of Daphne Caruana Galizia." https://www.theguardian.com/world/2017/oct/20/pope-writes-rare-letter-of-condolence-after-of-daphne-caruana-galizia.

Herbermann, Charles. *Hospitallers of St. John of Jerusalem: Catholic Encyclopedia*. New York: Robert Appleton Company, 1913.

Heydenreich, Ludwig. "Sculpture of Leonardo da Vinci." https://www.britannica.com/biography/Leonardo-da-Vinci/Sculpture#ref360267.

———. "Second Florentine period (1500–08) of Leonardo da Vinci." https://www.britannica.com/biography/Leonardo-da-Vinci/Second-Florentine-period-1500–08.

Hilliar, Andrew. "Brothers sentenced to 40 years in prison for murdering Maltese journalist Caruana Galizia." https://www.france24.com/en/europe/20221014-brothers-sentenced-to-40-years-in-prison-for-murdering-maltese-journalist-caruana-galizia.

Holland, Brynn. "The Knights Templar Rulebook Included No Pointy Shoes and No Kissing Mom." https://www.history.com/news/the-knights-templar-rulebook-included-no-pointy-shoes-and-no-kissing-mom.

Huls, Alexander. "Uncovering the Myths of Leonardo." https://magazine.krieger.jhu.edu/2023/05/uncovering-the-myths-of-leonardo/.

Hume, Edgar. *Medical Work of the Knights Hospitallers of Saint John of Jerusalem*. Baltimore: Johns Hopkins University Press, 1938.

ICIJ. "A new ICIJ investigation exposes a rogue offshore industry." https://www.icij.org/investigations/panama-papers/new-icij-investigation-exposes-rogue-offshore-industry/.

Independent. "Everyone can be Holy." https://www.independent.com.mt/articles/2008–07-06/local-news/Everyone-Can-be-holy-210023.

Iribarren, Marta. "Malta loses its commissioner nominee over hospital corruption scandal." https://www.euronews.com/health/2024/05/10/malta-loses-its-commissioner-nominee-to-corruption-scandal.

Isaacson, Walter. *Leonardo da Vinci*. New York City: Simon and Schuster, 2018.

Isenberg, Wesley. *The Gospel of Philip*. Leiden: E.J. Brill, 1996.

Itzkowitz, Laura. "10 Secrets of the Louvre, The World's Most Visited Museum." https://www.travelandleisure.com/attractions/museums-galleries/secrets-of-the-louvre-paris.

Jansen, Katherine. *The Making of the Magdalen: Preaching and Popular Devotion in the Later Middle Ages*. Princeton: Princeton University Press, 2001.

Jansson, Ida. "This has happened: The murder of Maltese journalist Daphne Caruana Galizia." https://www.svt.se/nyheter/utrikes/detta-har-hant-mordet-pa-journalisten-daphne-caruana-galizia.

Kemp, Martin. *Leonardo*. Oxford: Oxford University Press, 2004.

———. "Martin Kemp on the Prado Mona Lisa." https://www.arthistorynews.com/articles/1284_Martin_Kemp_on_the_Prado_Mona_Lisa.

Keshelava, Grigol. "Hidden Cardiovascular Anatomy in "Saint John the Baptist" by Leonardo da Vinci." https://pmc.ncbi.nlm.nih.gov/articles/PMC9357477/#:~:text=In%20our%20opinion%2C%20Leonardo%20da,carotid%20artery%2C%20left%20subclavian%20artery%2C%20C.

Kim, Young. *Epiphanius of Cyprus: Imagining an Orthodox World.* Ann Arbor: University of Michigan Press, 2017.

Kirchgaessner, Stephanie. "How Joseph Muscat's glittering political career lost its lustre." https://www.theguardian.com/politics/2018/apr/23/joseph-muscat-malta-political-career-lost-lustre.

Lambdin, Thomas. *Gospel of Thomas.* Milwaukee: Marquette University Press, 2020.

Lane-Pool, Stanley. *Saladin and the Fall of the Kingdom of Jerusalem.* London: G. P. Putnam's Sons, 1906.

Lebedev, Evgeny. "Caped crusaders: What really goes on at the Knights of Malta's secretive headquarters?" https://www.independent.co.uk/news/world/europe/caped-crusaders-what-really-goes-on-at-the-knights-of-malta-s-secretive-headquarters-9217469.html.

Lehrman. "Columbus reports on his first voyage, 1493." https://www.gilderlehrman.org/history-resources/spotlight-primary-source/columbus-reports-his-first-voyage-1493#:~:text=When%20Columbus%20arrived%20back%20in,in%20Latin%20by%20Stephan%20Plannck.

Liddell, Devin. "The Plague that Inspired Da Vinci to Design a City. We Should Steal His Idea." https://www.fastcompany.com/90163788/the-plague-inspired-da-vinci-to-design-a-city-we-should-steal-his-ideas.

Long, Keith. "The Synoptic Gospels & the Gospel of John: 7 Key Differences." https://www.bartehrman.com/thesynopticgospels/#:~:text=While%20the%20Synoptic%20Gospels%20begin,is%20the%20Miracle%2DMaker%20himself.

Macapia, Paul. "Charles d'Amboise." https://art.seattleartmuseum.org/objects/13470/charles-damboise#:~:text=The%20French%20nobleman%20Charles%20d,as%20he%20proudly%20demonstrates%20ohere.

Magri, Giulia. "Freemasons 'categorically' deny involvement in Daphne Caruana Galizia's murder." https://timesofmalta.com/article/freemasons-categorically-deny-involvement-in-daphne-caruana-galizias.875227.

———. "'Now we understand why Abela did not want the 'unexplained wealth order': Grech." https://timesofmalta.com/article/now-understand-abela-want-unexplained-wealth-order-grech.1088713.

Mairav, Zonszein. "Mideast's Largest Crusader-Era Hospital Unveiled." https://web.archive.org/web/20130808051440/http://news.nationalgeographic.com/news/2013/13/130805-archaeology-israel-jerusalem-crusader-middle-east-excavation/.

Malta. "Archbishop's Tenth Anniversary." https://orderofmalta.mt/2022/11/24/archbishops-tenth-anniversary/.

———. "Exchange of Greetings." https://orderofmalta.mt/2023/12/20/exchange-of-greetings/.

———. "Funeral of Fra' Matthew Festing in Malta." https://orderofmalta.mt/2021/12/03/funeral-of-fra-matthew-festing-in-malta/.

———. "Historic ties and shared projects: visit of Maltese (P)resident George Abela." https://www.orderofmalta.int/news/historic-ties-and-shared-projects-visit-of-maltese-mresident-george-abela/.

———. "Historical Legacy, Migration and Fort St. Angelo discussed during the Grand Master's State Visit to the Republic of Malta." https://www.orderofmalta.int/news/historical-legacy-migration-and-fort-st-angelo-discussed-during-the-grand-masters-state-visit-to-the-republic-of-malta/.

———. "Lourdes: the 53rd International pilgrimage of the Order of Malta." https://www. orderofmalta.int/news/lourdes-the-53rd-international-pilgrimage-of-the-order-of-malta/.

———. "The Great Siege of Malta 450 years ago." https://www.orderofmalta.int/news/ the-great-siege-of-malta-450-years-ago/.

Marie, André. "Mel Gibson's Upcoming Series on the Siege of Malta." https://catholicism. org/mel-gibsons-upcoming-series-on-the-siege-of-malta.html.

Martin, Sean. *The Knights Templar: The History & Myths of the Legendary Military Order.* New York: Thunder's Mouth, 2005.

McDonald, Patrick. "Prof says 'all hell broke loose' at Harvard after his study found no racial bias in police shootings." https://www.campusreform.org/article/ prof-says-all-hell-broke-loose-harvard-study-found-no-racial-bias-police shootings/24908?__hstc=135165998.4b44870ec4a577029c49e44b73bd3b ee.1734307200195.1734307200196.1734307200197.1&__hssc=135165998.1.1734 307200198&__hsfp=1473060762.

McKie, Robin. "'The situation has become appalling': fake scientific papers push research credibility to crisis point." https://www.theguardian.com/science/2024/feb/03/the-situation-has-become-appalling-fake-scientific-papers-push-research-credibility-to-crisis-point.

Melis, Alessandro. "Leonardo da Vinci designed an ideal city that was centuries ahead of its time." https://uk.news.yahoo.com/leonardo-da-vinci-designed-ideal-104442452. html?guccounter=1&guce_referrer=aHR0cHM6Ly93d3cuZ29vZ2xlLmNvbS88&g uce_referrer_sig=AQAAAGHHIXXnT6T8myfkeip2pXagwQJC5iWr7uOwKdhQB VqPRoOQtVZocEzW7TiPhUZ2CTqbXWpx32WbdIfYis6Gl1c9RpL72GIJvZWbiv WUwbcVUC2hwelb329IROmV079-nyrox-l1fNndY-yE3tplyopDe63MNcNCYG-sPIcGUsZj.

Menzies, Gavin. *1434: The Year a Chinese Fleet Sailed to Italy and Ignited the Renaissance.* London: Harper, 2009.

Merriam-Webster Dictionary. "Holy Grail." https://www.merriamwebster.com/diction ary/Holy%20Grail.

Missinne, Stefan. "Leonardo Depicted America: Misread as the Moon." https://www.scirp. org/journal/paperinformation?paperid=95063.

Morris, Roderick. "The Great Rustici Emerges from the Shadows." https://www.nytimes. com/2010/12/14/arts/14iht-conway14.html.

Museo Galileo. "Leonardo da Vinci and His Books: The Library of the Universal Genius." https://artsandculture.google.com/story/leonardo-da-vinci-and-his-books-museo-galileo/UAVRFMTE3VoqLg?hl=en.

Nardini, Bruno. *Fables of Leonardo da Vinci.* Northbrook: Hubbard, 1973.

Nicholson, Helen. *The Knights Templar: A New History.* Stroud: Sutton, 2001.

Orland, Kevin. "The 'da Vinci Globe': A chance discovery." https://www.independent. com.mt/articles/2021-11-28/local-news/The-da-Vinci-Globe-A-chance-discovery-6736238639.

Pace, Maria. "Malta's Explosive History: 19 Bomb Attacks Since 2010." https://www. maltatoday.com.mt/news/national/81438/maltas_explosive_history_19_bomb_ attacks_since_2010.

Paolucci, Antonio. *Il Battistero di San Giovanni a Firenze. The Baptistery of San Giovanni Florence (in Italian and English).* Modena: F.C. Panini, 1994.

———. *Michelangelo: Le Pietà.* Milan: Skira, 1997.

Pomella, Andrea. *Caravaggio: An Artist through Images.* Rome: ATS Italia Editrice, 2005.

Prata, Nicholas. *Angels in Iron.* Merchantville: Arx, 2004.

Price, Robert. *Deconstructing Jesus.* Buffalo: Prometheus, 2000.

———. "Iron John the Baptist." https://www.robertmprice.mindvendor.com/epi_ironjo. htm.

———. "Mary Magdalene: Gnostic Apostle?" https://www.robertmprice.mindvendor. com/art_mary_magdalene.htm.

———. *The Case Against the Case for Christ: A New Testament Scholar Refutes Lee Strobel.* Cranford: American Atheist Press, 2010.

———. *The Incredible Shrinking Son of Man: How Reliable Is the Gospel Tradition?* Buffalo: Prometheus, 2003.

———. "Was Jesus (and) John the Baptist Raised from the Dead?" https://robertmprice. mindvendor.com/art_jesus.htm#:~:text=He%20hath%20opened%20heaven's%20 door,No%20more%20fasting.

Quinones, Ricardo. ""Dante Alighieri—Biography, Poems, & Facts." https://www.bri tannica.com/biography/Dante-Alighieri.

Rankin, Jennifer. "Malta's former prime minister charged with corruption over hospital scandal." https://amp.theguardian.com/world/article/2024/may/09/maltas-former-prime-minister-charged-with-corruption-over-hospital-scandal.

———. "Suspect in Daphne Caruana Galizia murder says he got tipoffs from official." https://www.theguardian.com/world/2019/dec/05/malta-pm-joseph-muscat-not-convincing-over-resignation-delay-say-meps.

Reuters. "Malta grants pardon to suspected middleman in journalist murder—police sources." https://web.archive.org/web/20191125210336/https://uk.reuters.com/article /uk-malta-daphne/malta-grants-pardon-to-suspected-middleman-in-journalist-murder-police-sources-idUKKBN1XZ1TF.

Riley-Smith, Jonathan. *The Crusades, Christianity, and Islam.* New York: Columbia University Press, 2008.

———. *The Oxford Illustrated History of the Crusades.* Oxford: Oxford University Press, 1995.

Robinson, J.H. *The Decree Abolishing the Feudal System.* Boston: Ginn, 1906.

Rosenthal, Randy. ""Heaven and Hell': New history of the afterlife shows origins of the idea." https://www.jpost.com/israel-news/culture/heaven-and-hell-new-history-of-the-afterlife-shows-origins-of-the-idea-625613.

Royal Trust Collection. "Apocalyptic scenes, with notes c.1517–18." https://www.rct.uk/ collection/912388/apocalyptic-scenes-with-notes.

Rui, Andrea. "Santa Maria delle Grazie." https://www.unilibro.it/ebook/andrea-rui/santa-maria-grazie-e-book-pdf/83071208.

Sammut, Pierre. "Restoration work on central part of façade of St John's Co-Cathedral in Valletta complete." https://web.archive.org/web/20160314011159/http://www.in dependent.com.mt/articles/2015-09-04/local-news/Restoration-work-on-central-part-of-facade-of-St-John-s-Co-Cathedral-in-Valletta-complete-6736141610.

Schachterle, Joshua. "Who Was John the Baptist? (The Untold Story)." https://www. bartehrman.com/who-was-john-the-baptist/.

Segal, Muriel. *Painted Ladies: Models of the Great Artists.* New York City: Stein and Day, 1972.

Stern, Keith. *Queers in History: The comprehensive encyclopedia of historical gays, lesbians, and bisexuals.* Dallas: BenBella, 2009.

Stevenson, W.B. *The Crusaders in the East: A Brief History of the Wars of Islam with the Latins in Syria During the Twelfth and Thirteenth Centuries.* Cambridge: Cambridge University Press, 1907.

Strayer, Joseph. *The Reign of Philip the Fair.* Princeton: Princeton University Press, 1980.

Sugden, John. *Nelson: The Sword of Albion.* New York: Random House, 2014.

Tarbox, Wilson. "The Risky Business of Restoring Leonardos." https://hyperallergic.com/344691/the-risky-business-of-restoring-leonardos/.

The National Gallery. "Episode 4 | Infancy | Saint John the Baptist: From Birth to Beheading | National Gallery, London." YouTube, June 24, 2014, 0:52. https://www.youtube.com/watch?v=elscewC1g4k&t=5s.

Thomas-Akoo, Zak. "Ex-MGA CEO Farrugia found guilty of leaking secrets to Yorgen Fenech." https://next.io/news/regulation/heathcliff-farrugia-guilty-leaking-secrets/.

Tignor, Robert. *Worlds Together, Worlds Apart, Volume 1: Beginnings to the 15th Century.* New York: Norton, 2014.

Torre, Ignacio de la. *The Monetary Fluctuations in Philip IV's Kingdom of France and Their Relevance to the Arrest of the Templars.* In Jochen Burgtorf; Paul F. Crawford & Helen Nicholson (eds.). *The Debate on the Trial of the Templars (1307–1314).* Farnham: Ashgate, 2010.

Upton-Ward, Judith. *The Rule of the Templars.* Suffolk: Boydell, 1992.

Valantasis, Richard. *The Gospel of Thomas.* New York City: Routledge, 1997.

Vincent, Rebecca. "Malta: Seven years on, the murder of Daphne Caruana Galizia highlights continued need for reform." https://rsf.org/en/malta-seven-years-murder-daphne-caruana-galizia-highlights-continued-need-reform.

Wallace, Robert. *The World of Leonardo da Vinci: 1452–1519.* New York City: Time, 1966.

Weinstein, Donald. *Savonarola: The Rise and Fall of a Renaissance Prophet.* New Haven: Yale University Press, 2011.

Wertheim, Jon. "Inside the corruption allegations plaguing Malta." https://www.cbsnews.com/news/inside-the-corruption-allegations-plaguing-malta-60-minutes-2020–08-16/.

Xuereb, Matthew. "Konrad Mizzi has no regrets over acquisition of company in Panama; PM's chief also has Panama company, say reports." https://web.archive.org/web/20171016222644/https://www.timesofmalta.com/articles/view/20160228/local/konrad-mizzi-has-no-regrets-over-acquisition-of-company-in-panama.603936.

Zöllner, Frank. *Leonardo da Vinci: The Complete Paintings.* Cologne: Taschen, 2000.

www.ingramcontent.com/pod-product-compliance
Lightning Source LLC
Chambersburg PA
CBHW070342220526
45467CB00001B/215